The Alaska Cruise
Explorer

b   maker

Maps
Ports
Stories
Excursions

A favorite from my collection of historic Alaska photographs is this scene from Port Clarence, near the Arctic Circle, circa 1900. In the distance are seven steam whalers (two are behind the tent on the left) and two smaller schooners, the latter probably used for trading. You can clearly see six of the protected barrel-like crow's nests on the masts of the whalers.

In the foreground are two canvas tents next to a kayak, its hull made of caribou or seal skin stretched over a driftwood frame. Standing on the left-hand tent frame are what appear to be hoops of seal skin or perhaps whale blubber drying. On the post are some carved ivory figures.

There are few protected harbors in northwest Alaska, and this one on the Seward Peninsula not far from Nome was a favorite anchorage for whalers. A few years earlier, seven big whaling ships and their crews had become trapped in the ice near Point Barrow, farther north, and did not have enough food to get through the winter. They were saved by an expedition that drove a herd of reindeer from Port Clarence to Point Barrow, providing meat for the stranded whalers.

Opposite page: Old charts fascinate me. This is a portion of an 1895 chart with a hand-drawn line showing the Juneau-Sitka telegraph line that was laid along the bottom with all the splices noted. The journal is from my first trip to Alaska in my own boat.

The Alaska Cruise
Explorer

by Joe Upton, Mapmaker

So we came to Alaska on a wild and lost afternoon, caught in a tide race off a nameless point, far from any help. The heavy westerly swell, the dirty sou'west chop, and the push of the tide on top, it was all I could do just to keep way on the boat, throttling over the big ones and diving deep into the troughs. The seas came from all directions, and even at dead slow, waves slapped against the windows, sagging in the thick glass. Twice a green one poured in over the stern, filling the trolling cockpit, and the boat wallowed deep in the water until it drained. The shore wasn't far away and I looked long and hard at it. If the engine ever quit, we'd be broadside in a minute and probably swamp. If it came to that, I'd rather pour on the coal and put the bow in the trees. Even a rocky beach is better to walk home on than this crooked piece of water.

- My fishing journal, 1972

2014 Edition

Coastal Publishing
15166 Skogen Lane, Bainbridge Island, WA, 98110
Printed in Korea

Maps by Joe Upton

Photographs by Joe Upton unless noted with the following abbreviations:
AMNH - American Museum of Natural History, New York
AS - AlaskaStock
BCARS - British Columbia Archives and Records Service
BCRM- British Columbia Royal Museum
CRMM - Columbia River Maritime Museum, Astoria, Oregon
DK - Dan Kowalski
MOHAI - Museum of History and Industry, Seattle
SFM - San Francisco Maritime Museum
THS - Tongass Historical Society, Ketchikan, Alaska
UAF - University of Alaska, Fairbanks
UW - University of Washington Special Collections
WAT - Whatcom County (WA) Museum of History and Art

ISBN 978-0-9914215-0-3

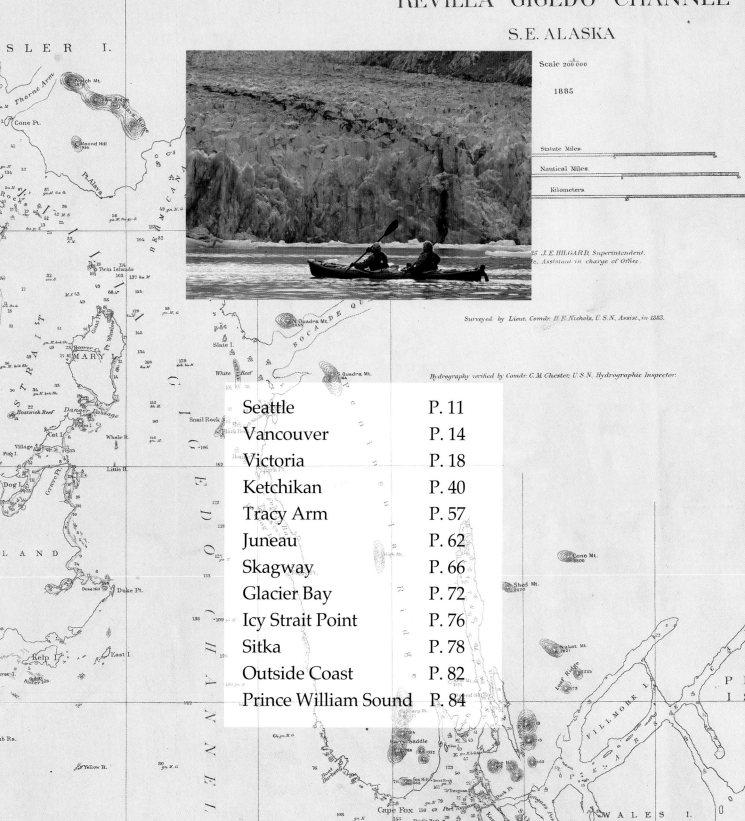

REVILLA GIGEDO CHANNEL

S.E. ALASKA

Scale 200 000

1885

Statute Miles.

Nautical Miles.

Kilometers.

J. E. HILGARD, Superintendent.
Assistant in charge of Office.

Surveyed by Lieut. Comdr. H. E. Nichols, U.S.N. Assist., in 1883.

Hydrography verified by Comdr. C. M. Chester, U.S.N. Hydrographic Inspector.

Seattle	P. 11
Vancouver	P. 14
Victoria	P. 18
Ketchikan	P. 40
Tracy Arm	P. 57
Juneau	P. 62
Skagway	P. 66
Glacier Bay	P. 72
Icy Strait Point	P. 76
Sitka	P. 78
Outside Coast	P. 82
Prince William Sound	P. 84

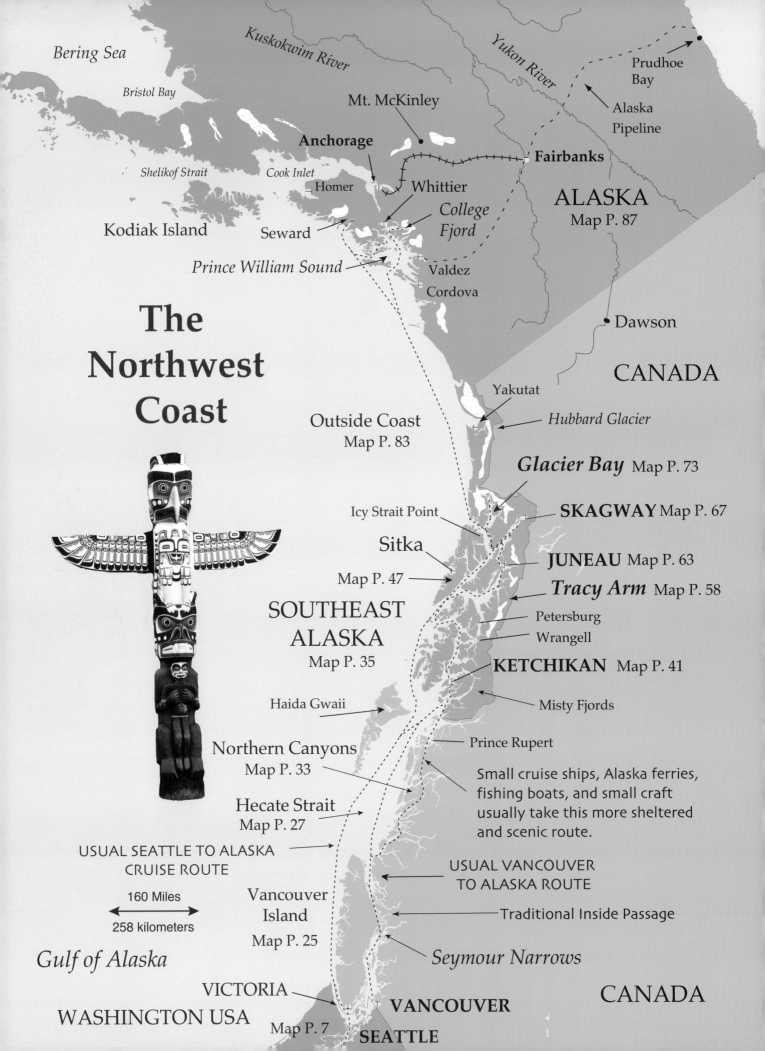

The Northwest Coast

Bering Sea

Bristol Bay

Kuskokwim River

Yukon River

Prudhoe Bay

Alaska Pipeline

Mt. McKinley

Anchorage

Fairbanks

Shelikof Strait

Cook Inlet

Homer

Whittier

College Fjord

ALASKA
Map P. 87

Kodiak Island

Seward

Valdez

Cordova

Prince William Sound

Dawson

CANADA

Yakutat

Hubbard Glacier

Outside Coast
Map P. 83

Glacier Bay Map P. 73

SKAGWAY Map P. 67

Icy Strait Point

Sitka

Map P. 47

JUNEAU Map P. 63

Tracy Arm Map P. 58

Petersburg

Wrangell

SOUTHEAST ALASKA
Map P. 35

KETCHIKAN Map P. 41

Misty Fjords

Haida Gwaii

Prince Rupert

Northern Canyons
Map P. 33

Small cruise ships, Alaska ferries, fishing boats, and small craft usually take this more sheltered and scenic route.

Hecate Strait
Map P. 27

USUAL SEATTLE TO ALASKA CRUISE ROUTE

USUAL VANCOUVER TO ALASKA ROUTE

160 Miles

258 kilometers

Vancouver Island
Map P. 25

Traditional Inside Passage

Gulf of Alaska

Seymour Narrows

CANADA

VICTORIA

WASHINGTON USA

Map P. 7

VANCOUVER

SEATTLE

To The Traveler

Mickey Hansen and me, Southeast Alaska, 1965. He showed me the ways of The North and filled my head with wonderful stories.

205

Video icon: Look for these icons on my maps, and go to www.joeupton.com to play the video.
Top Photo: DK.

When I was a green kid of 18, I had a powerful experience—working my first Alaska job on a fish-buying boat delivering salmon to a remote native cannery. Mickey Hansen, the grizzled Norwegian mate who had worked 50 seasons "up North," took me under his wing and shared with me the lore and legends of this vast region. That kindly old man was full of wonderful stories: "We went in there in the old *Mary A*, winter of '31. Thick o' snow, we'd toot that horn and listen for the echo off the rocks, through the snow." In this way, he instilled in me a passion for The North that I still have to this day.

For me, that long-ago summer of 1965 was ALASKA in capital letters. There were totems at the dock, eagles in the trees. All I wanted to do afterward was go up there to fish in my own boat.

Eventually I did, building a tiny waterfront cabin near a small roadless fishing settlement, too. Our little store/bar floated on logs. The bartender was the fish-buyer. You could sell your fish for bar credit and get right down to it with your neighbors. The choices were whiskey and water, whiskey and Coke, or whiskey and Tang. And he saved the ice for the fish.

For twenty years, I worked the coast in all kinds of boats, in all kinds of weather. I was a fish-buyer, a salmon fisherman, a king crab fisherman decades before "The Deadliest Catch."

When the wind blew, the anchor would go down and the rum bottle and the stories would come out.

When the big cruise ships started coming north, I designed a series of books with illustrated maps to share with these new visitors the drama and beauty of The North.

A few years ago, I started working with commercial fisherman/filmmaker Dan Kowalski. We'd take his boat to remote places and film short stories about what had happened there.

For me, the books and maps at first, and later the videos, were a way to share a sense of the mystery and the power of this place that is such a big part of my life.

So, come take this journey through a land that remains much as it was when the first explorers came through.

7

Puget Sound

Mile Zero of The Inside Passage begins in Seattle at Colman Dock. From here, thousands of gold-hungry men embarked on a journey to the Alaska and Klondike gold fields that changed so many lives in 1897 and 1898.

Look for the big ferries; they carry 2000 passengers and 220 cars from downtown Seattle to rural Bainbridge.

Mile 2 - Akli Beach... It was here that Seattle's first settlers, slogged ashore in a rainstorm in November 1851. The women of the party, who'd spent the previous six months struggling with the rigors of the Oregon Trail, broke into tears when they saw the promised land: a roofless cabin at the edge of a gloomy forest, a rough-looking Chief Sealth and members of his Suquamish tribe waiting to greet them.

Less than a month later, the sailing ship *Leonesa* dropped anchor, and her skipper offered the party $1,000 cash for a load of 50-foot fir piles. The settlers sharpened their axes and an industry was born.

Mile 9 - Tucked around the corner to the west is Port Madison, once site of one of the many big sawmills that used to dot most good Puget Sound harbors. They cut mostly big Doug fir, a beautifully grained, rot resistent wood that was shipped in big square riggers all over the world. Today, it is an exquisite little harbor surrounded with the fine homes of folks that mostly commute to Seattle.

Mile 18 - Over the bluff six miles east here is the engine that drove Puget Sound's economy during the 1960s and '70s, less so today: The Boeing Company, jet builder to the world. Today the big assembly building for the facility is home to the 747, 767, 777 and 787 Dreamliner production lines, and is the largest building by volume in the world.

Top: 14,409' Mt. Rainier looms near Seattle.
Right: Big square riggers loading giant Douglas fir timbers on Bainbridge Island around 1880. SFMM F12.21.725n

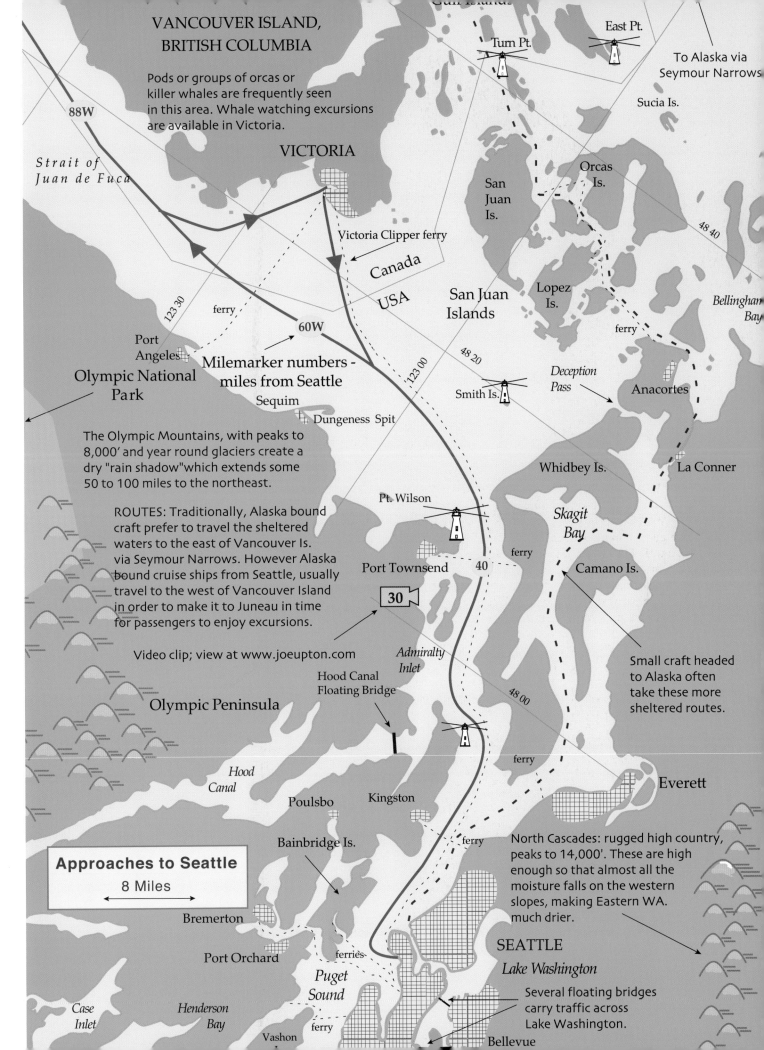

VANCOUVER ISLAND,
BRITISH COLUMBIA

Pods or groups of orcas or
killer whales are frequently seen
in this area. Whale watching excursions
are available in Victoria.

88W

*Strait of
Juan de Fuca*

VICTORIA

Victoria Clipper ferry

Canada

USA

San Juan
Islands

San
Juan
Is.

Orcas
Is.

Lopez
Is.

*Bellingham
Bay*

48 40

ferry

Turn Pt.

East Pt.

To Alaska via
Seymour Narrows

Sucia Is.

123 30

ferry

60W

Port
Angeles

Olympic National
Park

Milemarker numbers -
miles from Seattle

Sequim

Dungeness Spit

123 00

48 20

Smith Is.

*Deception
Pass*

Anacortes

La Conner

The Olympic Mountains, with peaks to
8,000' and year round glaciers create a
dry "rain shadow"which extends some
50 to 100 miles to the northeast.

Whidbey Is.

*Skagit
Bay*

ROUTES: Traditionally, Alaska bound
craft prefer to travel the sheltered
waters to the east of Vancouver Is.
via Seymour Narrows. However Alaska
bound cruise ships from Seattle, usually
travel to the west of Vancouver Island
in order to make it to Juneau in time
for passengers to enjoy excursions.

Pt. Wilson

ferry

Camano Is.

Port Townsend

40

Video clip; view at www.joeupton.com

30

*Admiralty
Inlet*

48 00

Small craft headed
to Alaska often
take these more
sheltered routes.

Hood Canal
Floating Bridge

Olympic Peninsula

ferry

Everett

*Hood
Canal*

Poulsbo

Kingston

Approaches to Seattle

8 Miles

Bainbridge Is.

ferry

North Cascades: rugged high country,
peaks to 14,000'. These are high
enough so that almost all the
moisture falls on the western
slopes, making Eastern WA.
much drier.

SEATTLE

Lake Washington

Bremerton

Port Orchard

ferries

*Puget
Sound*

Several floating bridges
carry traffic across
Lake Washington.

*Case
Inlet*

*Henderson
Bay*

ferry

Bellevue

Vashon

The Wild Olympic Peninsula

Wild is almost too tame a description for parts of the Northwest Coast. With very limited road access, long sections of the coast are totally isolated, only accessible by hiking through rough and thick forest. Nor are these shores particularly friendly when you actually get to them. In many places stretches of beach are cut off from the next beach by cliff-like headlands. At high tide, there may be no beach at all, but rather a jumble of driftwood that often includes large logs and whole trees, moving and surging with the waves that roll into it, creating a place where beachcombers could easily be injured or crushed.

There are spectacular hikes, particularly in the Hurricane Ridge area of Olympic National Park, south of Port Angeles. Farther west are some dramatic beach hikes. Shi Shi, near Neah Bay, and Rialto or First or Second beaches near La Push are accessible and very scenic.

Top: First Beach, near La Push DK
Above: Hikers in Olympic National Park
Right: Pacific Coast near Neah Bay

Exploring Seattle

Pike **Place Market** is probably the most varied food and craft market on the West Coast. It has several great places to eat overlooking the sound. Exciting!

Pioneer Square: This area of First Avenue at the southern end of downtown is an eclectic collection of galleries, shops, ethnic restaurants, the excellent Gold Rush Museum, and lots of street art. The highly recommended Seattle Underground Tour begins just off the square.

Seattle Art Museum: On First Avenue, in the heart of downtown, the museum just finished a major renovation. It offers many permanent and rotating collections. Highly recommended.

Fishermen's Terminal & Ballard Locks: Much of the Alaska fishing fleet, including some boats seen on "The Deadliest Catch," are based here.

Waterfront & Aquarium: Seattle's waterfront is a hopping place, a collection of shops, restaurants, and docks for excursion vessels. The Blake Island tour with a salmon dinner and Native American dancing is highly recommended. The latest addition to the waterfront is a large Ferris wheel with enclosed cars. If you ride on it in the long summer dusk, you'll get a super view across Puget Sound to the Olympic Mountains which rise to almost 8,000 feet.

Museum of Flight: Located next to Boeing Field, between downtown and Seattle-Tacoma International Airport, the museum features recent additions of stunning WWI and WWII dioramas.

Seattle Center: A popular attraction is the Experience Music Museum with its wonderful historical exhibits and hands-on activities, including an excellent section on Seattle's own wild and groovy Jimmy Hendrix. Another must-see attraction is the IMAX film of the Mount St. Helen's eruption, which shows several times a day at the Pacific Science Center.

Walk on the ferry: The Bainbridge ferry departs from downtown frequently during the day offering a 35-minute ride across Puget Sound. A 10-minute walk on the other side takes you to pleasant village of Winslow.

A few well-regarded restaurants in Seattle are Ivar's Acres of Clams, on the waterfront; McCormick & Schmick's, 1103 First Avenue; Anthony's Pier 66, waterfront; and Dragonfish Asian Café, 722 Pine Street.

11

The San Juan Islands

A place in the San Juans" is the ultimate dream for many Northwesterners—a little waterfront bungalow somewhere among the large and small islands of this sleepy archipelago, just 60 miles north of Seattle. With four major islands served by ferries out of Anacortes, and dozens of smaller ones, the San Juans are a major destination for vacationers and urbanites with second homes here.

Washington State has an excellent system of marine parks throughout Puget Sound and the San Juans, some on roadless islands with no ferry service. Many, many Washingtonians got their first taste of the islands as youths in one of the many summer camps, and just kept coming back as adults.

Opposite page: A lazy seal and a couple of classic six-meter sailboats, Orcas Island

Top: Turn Point Light, on Stuart Island, looks out at Boundary Pass and the Canadian Gulf Islands.

Above: A "Waterfront fixer-upper?" In your dreams! This is a cabin at Camp Four Winds on Orcas Island.

Left: Looking out at Reid Harbor, Stuart Island, one of the many excellent marine parks scattered through the islands.

Vancouver

Like most Northwest coast cities, forest products played a huge part in Vancouver's history, with big square riggers waiting to take lumber to Asian, Australian, and Pacific ports as soon as it could be milled. It still continues today – you'll cross the Fraser River entering the city by bus or car. Look down and most likely you'll see BC's premier product, logs, (some say marijuana is the biggest export...) traveling by barge or raft to a sawmill or a waiting ship.

With one of the best harbors on the coast, good road and rail connections, Vancouver quickly developed into Canada's premier west coast port as well. With a dramatic mountain and waterfront setting, the city became one of the favorite spots in the British Empire within a few decades of being founded, as evidenced by the many large and elegant Victorian era homes.

In more modern times, concerns about what would happen in Hong Kong after the mainland Chinese took over in 1997 led to the arrival of large numbers of Chinese immigrants, many of whom brought substantial personal wealth with them. The result is a noticeably multi-ethnic city with the second biggest Chinatown in North America.

Opposite page top: Early morning cruise ship approaches Canada Place.
Opposite middle left: Freighter and First Narrows Bridge
Opposite right: Shopping on Granville Island
Above: Tug and log raft, Vancouver, circa 1880. John Horton painting.
Left: Totems, Stanley Park, near Canada Place.

Victoria

While Vancouver—just 75 miles to the northwest—is a modern, cosmopolitan city with a heavy sprinkling of Asian immigrants, Victoria seems more like a taste of Olde England. The British fondness for gardens is especially evident in the many private and public gardens and plantings that line its streets.

Originally settled around a Hudson's Bay Company trading post established in 1843, this city and Vancouver Island became a crown colony in 1849. Ten years later, another colony was established on the mainland to support the many prospectors who had arrived with the 1858 Fraser River gold strike. Eventually the two colonies merged to form what is today British Columbia. Victoria became its capital, while Vancouver became the industrial center.

Victoria is a good place to shop for First Nations (coastal native) art and craft souvenirs. Many shops also specialize in goods from England that are hard to find elsewhere.

Because there are often orca or humpback whales in the vicinity, fast whale watching boats leave regularly from along the waterfront. Twelve miles from downtown Victoria is Butchart Gardens, one of the most popular attractions in the province. This stunning 50-acre showpiece had a rather humble beginning. In 1904, Jennnie Butchart, whose husband operated a nearby cement plant, got tired of staring at the ugly scar that his limestone quarrying operations left. She brought in a few plants to spruce up the area and one thing led to another.

Opposite page: The Empress Hotel dominates the Victoria waterfront.
Top: Totem near the Provincial Museum
Left: Statue in Butchart Gardens

17

" April 29, 1792. At four o'clock [a.m.] a sail was discovered to the westward standing in shore. This was a very great novelty, not having seen any vessel but our consort, during the last eight months."

The Explorer

This was a singular day for the British Captain George Vancouver and his two ships and crews. They had sailed from England 15 months earlier to seek the Northwest Passage from the Pacific Ocean to the Atlantic. Vancouver wasn't sure if it existed; he had been with Captain Cook when Cook had failed to find it.

The sail was Captain Robert Gray, a Boston fur trader, who pointed the way. Soon after, Vancouver discovered a channel 10 miles wide and 500 feet deep, leading east between high, snowy mountains. He thought it was the Northwest Passage. It wasn't.

At that time, Philadelphia and Boston had cobblestone streets and daily newspapers, yet the known world ended west of the Missouri River. Another 13 years would pass before Lewis and Clark would uncover the vastness and beauty of the American West.

A week after entering the unknown strait, the Vancouver party—continually charting and exploring, following the shore to make sure they missed no channel that might lead to the Atlantic—turned south and entered an unknown waterway Vancouver named for one of his lieutenants, Peter Puget. Vancouver was stunned by the beauty of what he saw.

When he arrived in Puget Sound and saw the myriad channels and passages leading off in all directions, it was obvious to Vancouver that the task of exploring was too difficult for his cumbersome ships, the *Discovery* and *Chatham*. The solution lay in using his 20-foot cutters, rigged to row and sail. The big boats would anchor while the small boats would set out, sometimes with Vancouver and sometimes without, charting the vast land they had discovered.

For three long summers, he explored, naming and charting much of the Northwest Coast. He lost just one man to shellfish poisoning. It was a remarkable feat.

Top: A painting by John Horton depicts Captain George Vancouver about to enter the Strait of Juan de Fuca.

Right: Part of Vancouver's map. Note that Glacier Bay (red circle) is mostly absent. It was full of ice!

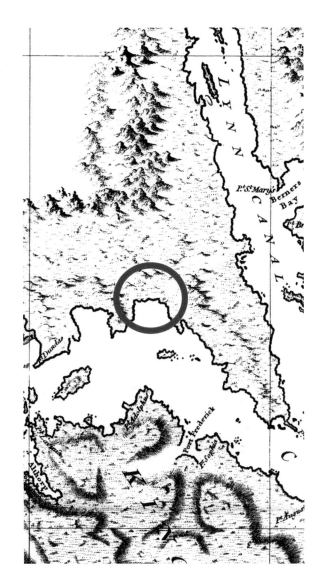

Northwest Tides

Tide Heights (feet)

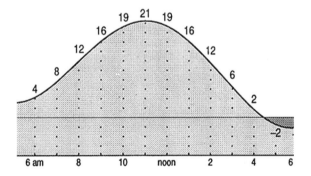

Imagine this: Several cubic miles of water must pass through the maze of narrow channels north of Vancouver every six hours as the tide moves in and out. This creates violent currents and whirlpools big enough to capsize 60-foot boats! The prudent mariner transits at slack water—near the time of high and low tide.

Once, when I was an incautious young skipper in a 60-footer, I was towing a disabled 36-foot fishing boat from Alaska to Seattle. Eager to get home, but having missed slack water, I thought I could get through constricted Dodd Narrows. So I went up onto the flying bridge and shouldered our way into the current.

Instantly I knew it was a mistake! The current shoved us violently back and forth and I was desperately afraid that the boat I was towing would hit the shore in one of our wild swings. Finally we got through, and I radioed back to the fellow I was towing, a cool customer, in his 25th season as an Alaska commercial fisherman.

"It wasn't too bad," he answered me, "I had to steer a bit to keep off the rocks. And I bit my cigar in half..."

Top: Channel marker near Petersburg in SE Alaska. On a big high tide, the water level would rise to the top of the marker. Six hours later, it would be 20 feet lower. This creates very swift currents, making for some very challenging maneuvering around the cannery docks.

Left, middle: Diagram shows around-the-clock rhythm of the tide.

Left, bottom: This kayaker is surfing on a standing wave in a tide rip at Skookumchuck Rapids, B.C., where the currents rush to almost 20 mph. For a dramatic video of a tugboat capsizing when the current pushes its barge ahead of it, check out: www.youtube.com/watch?v=QEfUblSDzww

Along the Way

ile 42: Point Wilson, about two and a half hours north of Seattle by cruise ship, is worth venturing onto the deck for. Here, the sheltered waters of Admiralty Inlet open up to the wider and rougher waters of the Strait of Juan de Fuca. About a half-mile to the south is the "Triangle of Fire," where three forts built around the entrance to Admiralty Inlet in Spanish-American War days (1899), could concentrate the fire of their big cannons. The big guns were removed long ago.

Port Townsend to the west and south of the lighthouse, is known for its many Victorian-era homes and buildings, a strong arts presence, and as the wooden boat center of the Northwest.

Mile 50W: Sequim rain shadow area. The high ridge of the Olympic Mountains serves to scrape the rain out of the storm systems sweeping in from the Pacific Ocean, creating a much drier and sunnier climate here than in surrounding areas.

Mile 60W: Orcas are often seen in these waters, particularly along the Vancouver Island shore. Keep your eyes peeled.

Mile 80W: Olympic National Park occupies much of the interior of the Olympic Peninsula south of here. With peaks rising to almost 8,000 feet, it has some of the most wild and remote country in the lower 48 states.

Mile 90W: A spot known as "one square inch of silence" is hidden in the Ho Rain Forest south of here. Found by sound researcher Gordon Hempton, it is believed to be one of the quietest places in the continental U.S.

Mile 120W: Cape Flattery is the most northwesterly corner of the continental U.S. The coast to the south of here is remote and rugged.

*Top: The cruise ship Oosterdam at Point Wilson, **Mile 42***
Right, top: Cape Flattery Lighthouse on tiny Tatoosh Island marks the entrance to the Strait of Juan de Fuca.
Right, bottom: A lapstrake skiff at Port Townsend, just south of Point Wilson

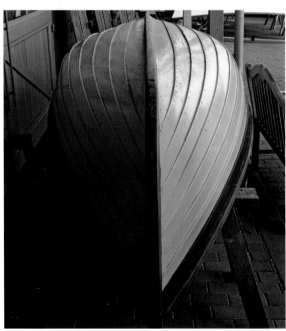

Inside vs. Outside Waters

To the mariner, "inside" basically means protected, away from the ocean waves and swells and effect of strong winds. When the Pleistocene glaciers carved out the canyons and fjords of the Northwest coast a million years ago, they created the Inside Passage and a future boater's paradise.

If there were no Inside Passage—if the coast of British Columbia and Alaska were like that of Oregon and California: bold terrain with great beaches but few harbors—there probably wouldn't be any Alaska cruises either, with no glacial fjords to cruise into or harbors to visit.

The very history of Alaska and British Columbia would have been much different, for it was the existence of all these sheltered passageways that allowed travelers, even in the smallest craft, to travel north in safety.

When cruise ships were small, say less than 500 feet long, they followed the traditional Inside Passage north of Vancouver Island to Alaska by way of Milbanke Sound, Lama Passage, Tolmie Channel, Graham and Fraser Reaches, and dramatic quarter-mile-wide Grenville Channel.

Unfortunately, almost all of today's very large ships find the traditional route a little too narrow. There are alternate wider but still scenic routes via Caamano Sound and Principe Channel. But for some reason, probably a minor cost saving—you don't need a Canadian pilot—most large ships now go straight up Hecate Strait from Vancouver Island to the Alaska border. It might be cheaper, but it isn't as scenic.

Top: Most of the outside coasts are rocky and exposed to the steady beat of Pacific surf. DK

Left, top: The sheltered inside passages between Vancouver Island and the mainland

Left, bottom: The crew of this schooner was lucky, surviving when their ship grounded on a beach instead of rocks. PSMHS 2727-3

The Wilderness Begins

Whether your ship leaves from Seattle, Vancouver, Seward, or Whittier, you transit that first night into essentially a vast wilderness—the wild north coast, with here and there a logging camp, Native settlement, or fishing town.

The transition is especially dramatic for passengers departing Vancouver. Late that first night or early the next morning, depending on the tide, you'll go through Seymour Narrows or, if on a small ship, Yuculta Rapids, in the Discovery Islands area. The tide runs so swiftly among these islands that even the largest vessels must wait for slack tide to continue through. To do otherwise risks getting shoved into the sides of the channel by the fast moving currents, or for smaller boats, being capsized by the powerful whirlpools.

Here, right at the spot where tidal rapids block the passage, where you must wait for the current to pause before you can pass safely, there is a dramatic transition from the settled south coast, with towns and lights along the shores, to the lonely north coast. North of here, there are few lights along the shore and for the most part no roads except around the very few towns.

It is almost as if nature had set a gate across the route. At the very place where the busy south coast ends and the wilderness begins. As if to warn the traveler of what lies beyond, as if simply to say: Watch out, be careful!

TIP: Evening and early-morning light along this coast can create a dramatic backdrop for photographs. Many of you have had a long day of travel to begin your cruise, and would love to sleep late on day two. But instead, consider getting up at six or earlier, grabbing your camera, and going out on the deck. The view could be spectacular.

Mighty Seymour

Every six hours, several cubic miles of water forces itself through quarter-mile-wide Seymour Narrows, **Mile 205**, as the tide pours in from the ocean. The current creates whirlpools big enough to suck small craft underwater. Safe passage is possible only in slack water at high and low tide.

It used to be much worse. A ship-killing rock once lurked underwater right at the narrowest spot, sinking about 80 ships before the rock was destroyed in 1958.

Blasting the underwater rock was an immense and hugely challenging project. At first, drillers worked from a barge anchored nearby with four 250-ton anchors! Didn't work. The current was too strong, moving the barge and breaking off the drills.

Finally, a huge tunneling project was undertaken—boring more than 3,200 feet of tunnels and vertical shafts reaching up into the interior of the rock. This was before the invention of sophisticated surveying equipment that we take for granted today. Drillers explored with small-diameter drills until they broke through to the water. Then, they'd plug the hole and use the information to create a three-dimensional map of where they were. Finally, tugs brought 2.8 million pounds of dynamite to fill the caverns and, and on April 7, 1958—adios, Ripple Rock!

All large cruise ships operating out of Vancouver and headed to and from Alaska pass through Seymour Narrows.

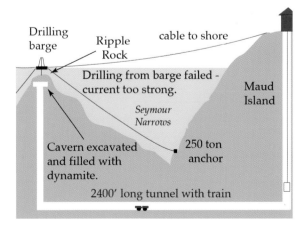

Top: Oosterdam passes right over where Ripple Rock used to lurk - right in narrowest part of Seymour Narrows.

Left, middle: The largest non-nuclear, man-made blast in history! Campbell River Museum

Left, bottom: This diagram shows that removal of Ripple Rock was a huge tunneling project, complete with elevators and a narrow-gauge railway.

Vancouver Island's Wild West Coast

Mile 120W-158W: Shipwreck Trail. Because so many vessels were wrecked here before electronic navigation, a rough trail was hacked out along this rugged coast. A cabin was built about every five miles and equipped with survival supplies, firewood, a telegraph with instructions for its operation in several languages, and directions for hiking out on the trail, Numerous crews were thrilled when they staggered ashore chilled, and often injured, to find a cabin with a woodstove and food.

Today it is called the West Coast Trail, with the reputation of being one of the most grueling treks in North America. It is isolated, physically challenging, and potentially hazardous. But hiking the trail is extremely rewarding due to the spectacular scenery and unique setting.

Mile 160W: The Bamfield Cable Station was where the undersea telegraph cable to Australia entered the ocean. A special ship had to be built from which to lay the 3,459-mile cable to Fanning Island in the mid-Pacific. From there the cable continued on to Australia.

Mile 195W: The many inlets and sounds in this area and farther north have become a major center for fish farming, employing many commercial fishermen looking for work after wild salmon runs declined in the 1980s.

Mile 220W: Nootka was a native village, home to the Nuu-chah-nulth people, where Britain and Spain agreed to a peaceable settlement to their conflicting territorial claims on the Northwest Coast. Sadly, First Nation tribes on Vancouver Island and elsewhere were decimated by diseases brought by Europeans.

Mile 260W: Ceepeecee (short for Canadian Packing Co.) at the head of Esperanza Inlet, was once a booming sardine cannery in the 1920s, '30s, and '40s. Today there are only ruins and a floating sport-fishing lodge.

Mile 290W: Cape Cook. More than one couple wanting to head for the South Pacific in their sailboat decided to take a "shakedown cruise" around Vancouver Island. Big mistake. The weather here can be worse than any they would find in mid-ocean,and after a taste of nasty weather, some decided to abandon the whole idea.

Mile 310W: Triangle Island was the site of an ill-fated lighthouse built in 1910 on top of a 600-foot cliff. The site proved too foggy and windy. Buildings had to be held down with cables least they be blown off the cliffs. Now home to millions of seabirds.

Top: Sign of the new economy. After logging was cut back and fishing slowed, the surfers and kayakers and Vancouver families seeking affordable second homes came to transform the economy.

Above: Logging crew and steam locomotive. These guys were lucky—they had a train. Most of the west coast of Vancouver Island was too rough and remote for trains to reach. UW 10564

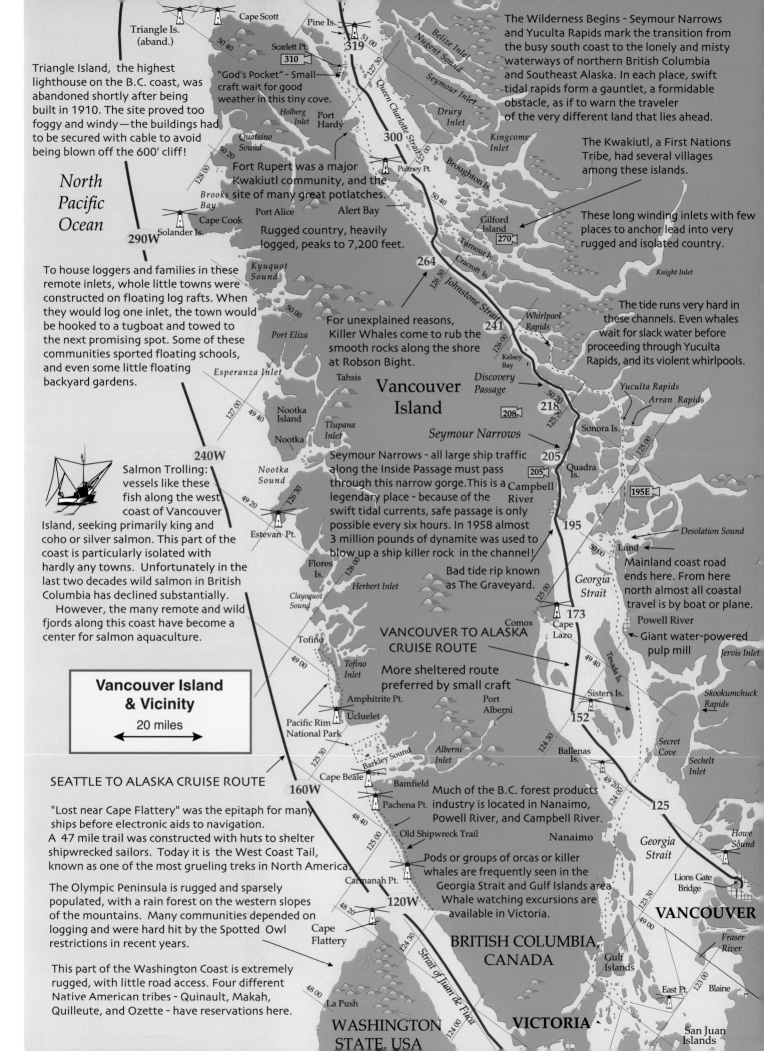

Triangle Is. (aband.)

Cape Scott

Pine Is.

319

51 00

50 40

Scarlett Pt.

310

127 00

Belize Inlet

Nugent Sound

Seymour Inlet

The Wilderness Begins - Seymour Narrows and Yuculta Rapids mark the transition from the busy south coast to the lonely and misty waterways of northern British Columbia and Southeast Alaska. In each place, swift tidal rapids form a gauntlet, a formidable obstacle, as if to warn the traveler of the very different land that lies ahead.

Triangle Island, the highest lighthouse on the B.C. coast, was abandoned shortly after being built in 1910. The site proved too foggy and windy—the buildings had to be secured with cable to avoid being blown off the 600' cliff!

"God's Pocket" - Small craft wait for good weather in this tiny cove.

Holberg Inlet

Port Hardy

Queen Charlotte Strait

Drury Inlet

Kingcome Inlet

The Kwakiutl, a First Nations Tribe, had several villages among these islands.

North Pacific Ocean

Quatsino Sound

50 20

128 00

300

Pultney Pt.

127 00

Broughton Is.

50 40

Fort Rupert was a major Kwakiutl community, and the site of many great potlatches.

Brooks Bay

Cape Cook

Solander Is.

Port Alice

Alert Bay

Gilford Island

270

These long winding inlets with few places to anchor lead into very rugged and isolated country.

290W

Rugged country, heavily logged, peaks to 7,200 feet.

Turnour Is.

Cracroft Is.

264

126 30

Johnstone Strait

Knight Inlet

To house loggers and families in these remote inlets, whole little towns were constructed on floating log rafts. When they would log one inlet, the town would be hooked to a tugboat and towed to the next promising spot. Some of these communities sported floating schools, and even some little floating backyard gardens.

Kyuquot Sound

50 00

Port Eliza

For unexplained reasons, Killer Whales come to rub the smooth rocks along the shore at Robson Bight.

Whirlpool Rapids

241

126 00

The tide runs very hard in these channels. Even whales wait for slack water before proceeding through Yuculta Rapids, and its violent whirlpools.

Esperanza Inlet

127 00

49 40

Tahsis

Kelsey Bay

Discovery Passage

50 20

218

125 30

Yuculta Rapids

Arran Rapids

Nootka Island

Vancouver Island

Nootka

Tlupana Inlet

Seymour Narrows

208

Sonora Is.

125 00

240W

Salmon Trolling: vessels like these fish along the west coast of Vancouver Island, seeking primarily king and coho or silver salmon. This part of the coast is particularly isolated with hardly any towns. Unfortunately in the last two decades wild salmon in British Columbia has declined substantially.

Nootka Sound

49 20

126 30

Seymour Narrows - all large ship traffic along the Inside Passage must pass through this narrow gorge. This is a legendary place - because of the swift tidal currents, safe passage is only possible every six hours. In 1958 almost 3 million pounds of dynamite was used to blow up a ship killer rock in the channel!

205

205

Quadra Is.

Campbell River

195E

Estevan Pt.

Flores Is.

126 00

Herbert Inlet

Bad tide rip known as The Graveyard.

195

50 00

Lund

Desolation Sound

Mainland coast road ends here. From here north almost all coastal travel is by boat or plane.

However, the many remote and wild fjords along this coast have become a center for salmon aquaculture.

Clayoquot Sound

VANCOUVER TO ALASKA CRUISE ROUTE

Georgia Strait

Powell River

Tofino

More sheltered route preferred by small craft

125 00

173

Comox

Cape Lazo

Giant water-powered pulp mill

Jervis Inlet

Tofino Inlet

49 00

Amphitrite Pt.

Ucluelet

Port Alberni

49 40

Tesada Is.

Skookumchuck Rapids

Vancouver Island & Vicinity

20 miles

Pacific Rim National Park

125 30

Sisters Is.

152

124 30

Secret Cove

Barkley Sound

Alberni Inlet

Ballenas Is.

124 30

124 00

Sechelt Inlet

Cape Beale

Bamfield

125

SEATTLE TO ALASKA CRUISE ROUTE

160W

Pachena Pt.

48 40

Much of the B.C. forest products industry is located in Nanaimo, Powell River, and Campbell River.

49 20

Howe Sound

"Lost near Cape Flattery" was the epitaph for many ships before electronic aids to navigation. A 47 mile trail was constructed with huts to shelter shipwrecked sailors. Today it is the West Coast Tail, known as one of the most grueling treks in North America.

Old Shipwreck Trail

125 00

Nanaimo

Lions Gate Bridge

The Olympic Peninsula is rugged and sparsely populated, with a rain forest on the western slopes of the mountains. Many communities depended on logging and were hard hit by the Spotted Owl restrictions in recent years.

Carmanah Pt.

Pods or groups of orcas or killer whales are frequently seen in the Georgia Strait and Gulf Islands area. Whale watching excursions are available in Victoria.

Georgia Strait

123 30

VANCOUVER

This part of the Washington Coast is extremely rugged, with little road access. Four different Native American tribes - Quinault, Makah, Quilleute, and Ozette - have reservations here.

48 20

120W

Cape Flattery

124 30

BRITISH COLUMBIA, CANADA

Fraser River

123 00

La Push

48 00

Strait of Juan de Fuca

124 00

49 00

VICTORIA

East Pt.

Blaine

WASHINGTON STATE, USA

Gulf Islands

San Juan Islands

Hecate Strait Can Get Nasty

Hecate Strait is the least "inside" part of the Inside Passage. Many big cruise ships steam right up the middle of the strait, as it is the fastest and easiest way to Alaska. For most of the way, you are almost out of sight of land. Often all you will see are the tops of the mountains on Haida Gwaii to the west. Large ships traveling this route in the summer usually have a smooth trip.

Even if you encounter a typical summer blow, seas that would make uncomfortable traveling for a 30- to 60-foot yacht or fishing boat would barely bother your big ship.

Before cruise ships got so big, they usually took the traditional Inside Passage route–the heavy dotted line on the map. But the very large ships found the tight turn at **Boat Bluff Lighthouse, Mile 439**, to be too difficult to make safely, and residents in **Bella Bella, Mile 400**, objected to the big ships passing there, so alternate routes were sought. Sometimes they would travel via Johnson Return Channel or Principe Channel.

Sadly, what I have observed recently is that most captains take the easy way–straight up boring, wide Hecate Strait. So, if your ship goes up one of the narrower channels, tell your captain how much you appreciated it and mention it in your comment cards.

Winter passages here are quite a different story. On one big Alaska ferry a truck broke loose from its chain tie-downs on the car deck and slid back and forth, smashing cars and campers on all sides. When the ferry finally pulled into Ketchikan, a wrecker had to come aboard to pull the smashed cars out and they were lucky there was no fire or dead pets.

Top: A nasty trip in our 104' steel crabber, Flood Tide, in March, 1971. We encountered a tide rip so bad we didn't dare cross it.

*Right, middle: A 36-footer battles a June storm near **Mile 320**. This boat with a family and two kids in diapers had been waiting for better weather at Safety Cove, **Mile 354**, but when they ran out of diapers they figured it was time to go for it.*

Right, bottom: This is a typical day in Hecate Strait in summer–calm.

But usually not for cruise ships..

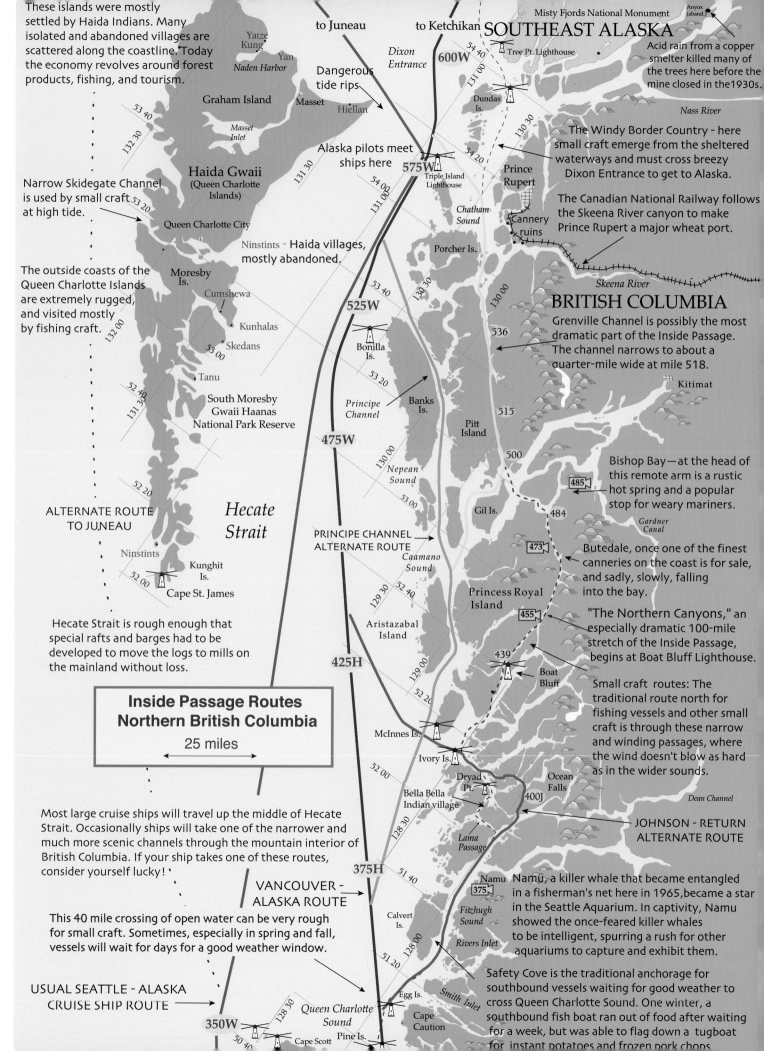

These islands were mostly settled by Haida Indians. Many isolated and abandoned villages are scattered along the coastline. Today the economy revolves around forest products, fishing, and tourism.

Yatze Kung

Yan
Naden Harbor

Graham Island

Masset
Hiellan

Masset Inlet

Haida Gwaii
(Queen Charlotte Islands)

Narrow Skidegate Channel is used by small craft at high tide.

Queen Charlotte City

Ninstints - Haida villages, mostly abandoned.

Moresby Is.

Cumshewa

The outside coasts of the Queen Charlotte Islands are extremely rugged, and visited mostly by fishing craft.

Kunhalas

Skedans

Tanu

South Moresby Gwaii Haanas National Park Reserve

Hecate Strait

ALTERNATE ROUTE TO JUNEAU

Ninstints

Kunghit Is.

Cape St. James

Hecate Strait is rough enough that special rafts and barges had to be developed to move the logs to mills on the mainland without loss.

**Inside Passage Routes
Northern British Columbia**

25 miles

Most large cruise ships will travel up the middle of Hecate Strait. Occasionally ships will take one of the narrower and much more scenic channels through the mountain interior of British Columbia. If your ship takes one of these routes, consider yourself lucky!

This 40 mile crossing of open water can be very rough for small craft. Sometimes, especially in spring and fall, vessels will wait for days for a good weather window.

USUAL SEATTLE - ALASKA CRUISE SHIP ROUTE

350W

128 30

50 40

Cape Scott

Queen Charlotte Sound

Pine Is.

---

to Juneau

to Ketchikan SOUTHEAST ALASKA

Dixon Entrance

600W

Tree Pt. Lighthouse

Misty Fjords National Monument

Anyox (aband.)

Acid rain from a copper smelter killed many of the trees here before the mine closed in the 1930s.

Dangerous tide rips

Masset

Alaska pilots meet ships here

575W

Triple Island Lighthouse

Dundas Is.

Nass River

The Windy Border Country - here small craft emerge from the sheltered waterways and must cross breezy Dixon Entrance to get to Alaska.

Prince Rupert

Chatham Sound

Cannery ruins

The Canadian National Railway follows the Skeena River canyon to make Prince Rupert a major wheat port.

Porcher Is.

525W

Bonilla Is.

Principe Channel

Banks Is.

Skeena River

BRITISH COLUMBIA

Grenville Channel is possibly the most dramatic part of the Inside Passage. The channel narrows to about a quarter-mile wide at mile 518.

536

Kitimat

475W

Nepean Sound

Pitt Island

515

500

Bishop Bay—at the head of this remote arm is a rustic hot spring and a popular stop for weary mariners.

485

484

Gil Is.

Gardner Canal

PRINCIPE CHANNEL ALTERNATE ROUTE

Caamano Sound

473

Butedale, once one of the finest canneries on the coast is for sale, and sadly, slowly, falling into the bay.

425H

Aristazabal Island

455

Princess Royal Island

"The Northern Canyons," an especially dramatic 100-mile stretch of the Inside Passage, begins at Boat Bluff Lighthouse.

439

Boat Bluff

Small craft routes: The traditional route north for fishing vessels and other small craft is through these narrow and winding passages, where the wind doesn't blow as hard as in the wider sounds.

McInnes Is.

Ivory Is.

Dryad Pt.

Ocean Falls

400J

Bella Bella Indian village

Lama Passage

Dean Channel

JOHNSON - RETURN ALTERNATE ROUTE

375H

VANCOUVER - ALASKA ROUTE

Namu

375

Fitzhugh Sound

Calvert Is.

Rivers Inlet

Namu, a killer whale that became entangled in a fisherman's net here in 1965, became a star in the Seattle Aquarium. In captivity, Namu showed the once-feared killer whales to be intelligent, spurring a rush for other aquariums to capture and exhibit them.

Egg Is.

Smith Inlet

Cape Caution

Safety Cove is the traditional anchorage for southbound vessels waiting for good weather to cross Queen Charlotte Sound. One winter, a southbound fish boat ran out of food after waiting for a week, but was able to flag down a tugboat for instant potatoes and frozen pork chops.

Looking For Whales

Top: *School of orcas in Johnstone Strait, B.C. Their tall dorsal fins and black and white markings make them easy to identify.* Minden Pictures

Left, middle: A humpback lifts his tail before diving, as seen on a Juneau whale-watching tour.

*Left bottom: A dramatic humpback breach in Frederick Sound, Alaska, near **Mile 845**, photographed by commercial fisherman Duncan Kowalski.*

Want to see whales? Just keep your binoculars with you. Whales, particularly humpbacks, are seen all along the Northwest coast. And they're easy to find.

Whales are mammals, meaning they need to breathe on the surface. When they do, they exhale dramatically, creating a spout of water mixed with air that can be seen for miles, as in "Thar she blows."

Typically, whales will linger on the surface, breathing slowly, usually making shallow short dives between breaths. Then, when they lift their tail like the whale is doing in the middle picture to the left, it means that the whale will be "sounding," or diving deep, and may be down for as long as 15 minutes before coming up the surface again.

If you are lucky, you'll see a breach like the bottom photo in which a humpback jumps clear of the water and lands with a terrific splash that may be seen for miles. It's not clear why they do this. Perhaps they are dislodging parasites.

You also may see bubble-feeding, when a group of humpbacks will circle a school of herring, breathing to create a fence of bubbles, then surface dramatically through the school with their mouths open.

Orcas, or "killer" whales, are the other commonly seen whale. These are smaller, up to 30 feet, but are easily recognized by their tall scimitar-like dorsal fins. They are aggressive feeders, chowing down on salmon, seals, sea lions, and sometimes even smaller whales.

Ghost Canneries of The B.C. Coast

In the 1920s, 30s, and 40s, the Union Steamship vessels would load up with native and white laborers in Southern British Columbia, and head north. To dozens and dozens of canneries scattered along the B.C. Coast, sleeping away the winter with just a caretaker, but coming to life as the salmon season approached.

Rivers Inlet had six canneries, the Skeena River had more than twenty. Some were tiny one line operations that only lasted a few seasons. Others like Butedale, right, were whole little towns that operated for decades. First came consolidation as big canneries took over little ones, absorbing their fishermen. Next came the development of refrigerated transport vessels that allowed fish to be moved long distances to towns where a cannery could operate more cheaply.

Then came overfishing, poor management, a landslide at Hell's Canyon on the mighty salmon producing Fraser River, and poor logging practises.

The result is that today the BC salmon industry is but a shadow of what it once was, with ghost towns and just pilings on the beaches where canneries used to prosper.

Top: Redonda Bay, 1972.
Upper right: Butedale, 1997, slowly falling into the bay.
Lower right; North Pacific Cannery, near Prince Rupert is now a visitor attraction.

Top: The venerable Princess May aground on Sentinel Island, north of Juneau, in 1910. Amazingly, she survived with little damage. But her escape may have led the captain of the Princess Sophia, which grounded a few miles away in a snowstorm in 1918, to decline an offer to transfer his passengers to rescue craft. Tragically, the Sophia's fate was very different. The storm blew her off the reef in the middle of the following night, and all 343 aboard perished in the worst marine disaster in Alaska history. PSMHS Williamson 2074-10

Above: Gillnetter in Grenville channel. Need water? The shore is so steep here that you could be in deep water and let the waterfall fill your tanks!

Right: Part of the Hansen Handbook, which allowed users to travel to Alaska without charts or GPS, as long as you followed it exactly.

Channel	Seattle to Ketchikan Via Active Pass and Inside	Port or Stbd. Beam	Dist. off Miles
	Sainty (Camp) Pt. Lt. (22 ft. 10 mi.) Fl. W.	S	½
	{Union Passage, South point {East shore	P S	3/8 3/8
	James Pt. North entrance Lowe Inlet. To anchor in Lowe Inlet enter mid-channel on course 611° true, 343° mag.; when 0.4 mi. inside Pt. Hepburn, round Don Pt. to course 047° true, 019° mag., heading on David Pt. for 0.5 mi. to anchorage in 20 fathoms. Strong tidal currents across entrance, flooding northward and ebbing southward. Lowe Inlet.	S	¼
	Tom Id. Bn. On islet 0.2 mi. N.W. of Lowe Inlet.	S	⅛
	Mountain (Ormiston) Pt. Lt. (15 ft. 8 mi.) Fl. W. On east shore of Pitt Id. on west side of channel.	P	1/10
	Serpent Waterfall Approximate mid-channel position.	P	¼
	Waterfall No. 2	P	3/16
	Knewnuggit Lt. (20 ft. 10 mi.) Fl. W.	S	¼

(Grenville Channel)

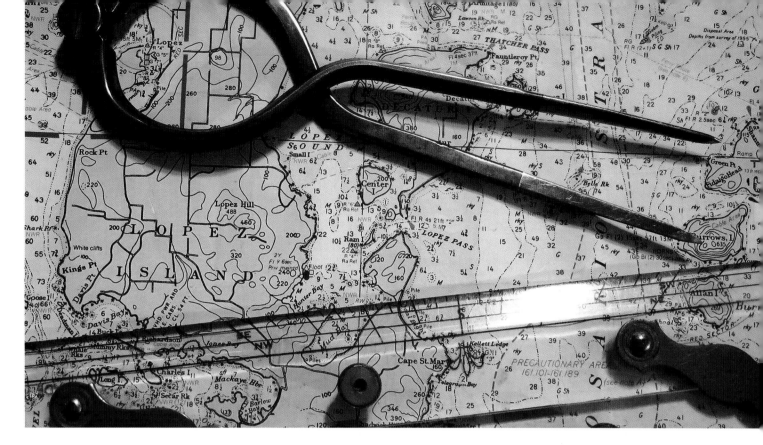

Navigation In The iPad Era

It used to be when you went north with a boat, you'd have to bring a stack of charts, or at the least two or three heavy spiral-bound chartbooks, plus two tide books–one for Canada, and another for the U.S.—plus dividers, parallel rulers, and Coast Pilots (textbook-like guidebooks). Plus, you'd need space to unfold the big charts. This was all very challenging on a typical small boat.

Today that is so Old School. That heavy stack of charts has in most vessels been replaced by a chart-plotter, a device that receives a GPS signal from satellites and displays your position in real time as an icon on a moving chart. In recent, years, apps for the iPad, iPhone, and other devices do the same thing.

Recently I took a 10-day trip with friends to the islands that straddle the Canada–Washington border. The app on my iPhone, which cost $10, was more accurate than the dedicated GPS plotter on board.

The GPS on the iPhone is from Navionics, available at the App Store. It's a great way to follow your route and compare it with the maps in this book.

Top: Lopez Pass, San Juan Islands, is seen on a paper chart with dividers for measuring distance and parallel rulers for determining a boat's course.

Right: Screens of the same area on iPad (top) and iPhone (bottom). The little triangle on the iPad screen shows the position of the user's boat.

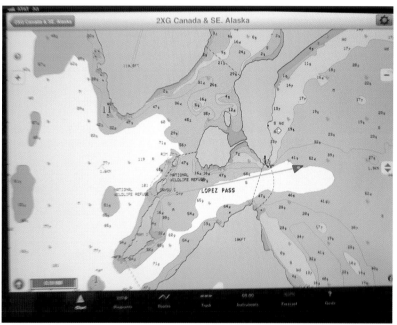

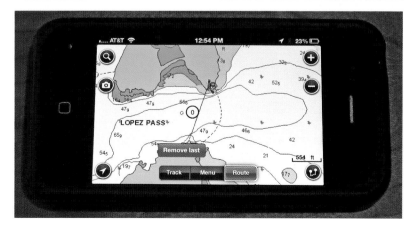

Through The Northern Canyons

Top: Captain Turner takes the Zuiderdam through Grenville Channel in May, 2012.
Left, middle: Grenville Channel seen from an Alaska Airlines flight
Left, bottom: Looking up into Grenville Channel

Grenville Channel, **Mile 500** to **Mile 546**, is one of the most scenic of the routes used by big ships. If your ship goes through there, consider yourself lucky, as most captains avoid it, perhaps because of what is called the Concordia Syndrome in the cruise industry. This is a risk-avoidance strategy based on what happened when the captain of an Italian cruise ship crashed his ship into a rock, killing 32, in 2012.

The channel, however, is used by almost all smaller craft headed north or south along the coast. It is very deep and only about 1,200 feet wide in the narrowest spot.

This is part of the Inside Passage that I have nicknamed The Northern Canyons that starts at Boat Bluff Lighthouse, **Mile 310,** and runs for almost 200 miles through Tolmie Channel, Graham and Fraser Reaches, across many-armed Wright Sound and into Grenville. Traveling this stretch truly seems like winding deep through the mountain heart of British Columbia.

Even though it is sheltered and protected, the channel has not been without tragedy. On a black March night in 2006, around midnight, the big B.C. ferry, *Queen of the North*, a critical link between the mainland and the Haida Gwaii Islands, rammed Gil Island and sank, taking two passengers with it. The cause was human error. The officer who had been on watch at the time was fired and went to jail after a lengthy trial.

The traditional Inside Passage, used by large and small craft for generations, follows the sheltered passages deep through the mountainous interior of British Columbia.

This area is almost complete wilderness except for the First Nations villages at Klemtu and Bella, and the semi-abandoned canneries at Namu, **Mile 375**, and Butedale, **Mile 473**.

But before over fishing and poor logging practises decimated the strong salmon runs along the coast, this area was home to almost 40 salmon canneries large and small. Each spring the steamers of the Union Steamship Company would bring thousands of workers from the cities of lower British Columbia to the canneries to catch and process fish. Natives would often paddle for days in canoes made of huge cedar logs to work in the canneries as well.

And it was along these steep sided inlets that the handloggers flourished in the days before chainsaws and heavy logging equipment. They would seek big cedars and spruces, that when expertly cut, would slide all the way down into the salt water, where they would form a raft with others and eventually be towed to the mills at Swanson Bay and Ocean Falls.

Top: Your mapmaker and crew take a break at the Bishop Bay Hot Springs, east of **Mile 484,** *after a long hard season in The North.*

Lower: Somewhere in the Northern Canyons, a fish buyer drops the anchor for the night.

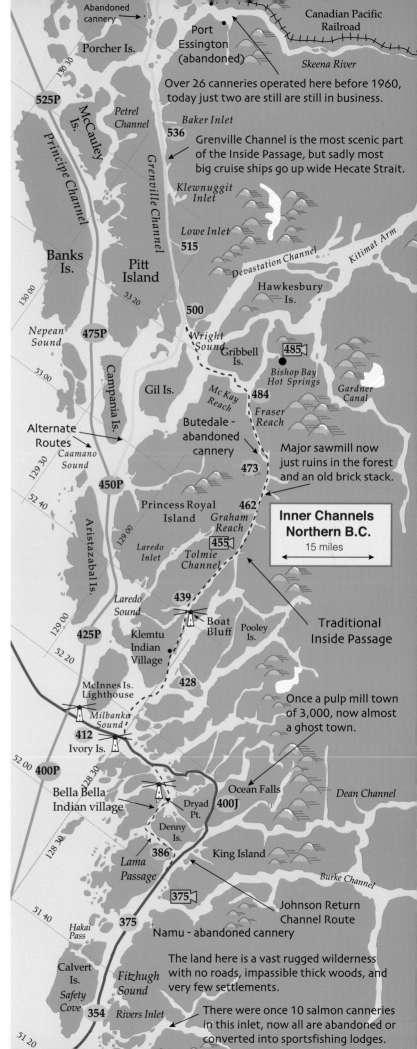

Porcher Is.

Abandoned cannery

Canadian Pacific Railroad

Port Essington (abandoned)

Skeena River

Over 26 canneries operated here before 1960, today just two are still are still in business.

536

Baker Inlet

Grenville Channel is the most scenic part of the Inside Passage, but sadly most big cruise ships go up wide Hecate Strait.

Klewnuggit Inlet

McCauley Is.

525P

Petrel Channel

Principe Channel

Grenville Channel

Lowe Inlet

515

Devastation Channel

Kitimat Arm

Banks Is.

Pitt Island

500

Hawkesbury Is.

Wright Sound

Gribbell Is.

485

Bishop Bay Hot Springs

Nepean Sound

475P

Gil Is.

McKay Reach

484

Gardner Canal

Campania Is.

Fraser Reach

Butedale - abandoned cannery

Major sawmill now just ruins in the forest and an old brick stack.

473

Alternate Routes

Caamano Sound

450P

Princess Royal Island

462

Graham Reach

455

Inner Channels Northern B.C.
← 15 miles →

Laredo Inlet

Tolmie Channel

Aristazabal Is.

439

Boat Bluff

Pooley Is.

Traditional Inside Passage

Laredo Sound

425P

Klemtu Indian Village

428

Once a pulp mill town of 3,000, now almost a ghost town.

McInnes Is. Lighthouse

Milbanke Sound

412

Ivory Is.

400P

Bella Bella Indian village

Ocean Falls

Dean Channel

Dryad Pt.

400J

Denny Is.

386

King Island

Lama Passage

Burke Channel

375

Johnson Return Channel Route

Hakai Pass

375

Namu - abandoned cannery

The land here is a vast rugged wilderness with no roads, impassible thick woods, and very few settlements.

Calvert Is.

Safety Cove

Fitzhugh Sound

354

Rivers Inlet

There were once 10 salmon canneries in this inlet, now all are abandoned or converted into sportsfishing lodges.

SOUTHEAST ALASKA:
A Man and a Boat Could Travel For Weeks and Never Find a Town

The coast of Alaska, like British Columbia, is deeply indented with inlets winding far back into the mountainous and forbidding interior. The islands, large and small, form a maze of channels. In the northern part, glaciers lay at the head of many of the inlets, discharging ice year round.

Most of the area is thickly forested, without settlements or towns, little changed since the arrival of the white man. Almost all the land is owned by federal and state governments; little is available for sale to individuals.

There are a few small towns. Each has a few miles of roads, few are connected to each other or to the "outside." Most travel is by boat or plane.

Scattered in little coves and harbors far from the towns are a few roadless communities that still enjoy a quiet existence. Except for storekeepers and the fish-buyers, residents mostly fish for salmon. In summer, they scatter up and down the coast, hustling to make a year's pay in a few months.

Then comes the fall. The outside boats straggle back to Washington, the days get shorter, and the sun disappears behind thick clouds. Weeks pass with only an occasional boat or float plane arriving to break the monotony.

Despite short days and gloomy weather, many local residents prefer winter. After the rush of the salmon season, winter can be a welcome change with time to work on cabin or boat, visit with neighbors, or just sit and read. It's not a fast-paced life, but there's enough to do. Many residents have spent time in the larger towns and wouldn't think of moving back.

Top: Ice from Le Conte Glacier east of Petersburg, sometimes drifts into upper Frederick Sound, creating a hazard to mariners. The old Emily Jane, which my wife and I operated as a fish-buying vessel in 1981-82, hit an iceberg just north of Petersburg in 2009. The quick-thinking skipper ran her into shallow water before she sank, and no one was hurt.

Right: On the docks at Wrangell

SOUTHEAST ALASKA
Points of Interest:

1. Glacier Bay: In 1794, the first white man to come here, English explorer George Vancouver, found no bay, just solid ice all the way out to Icy Strait.

2. Lynn Canal: Surrounded by high mountains and glaciers, this waterway can be a fierce wind tunnel.

3. Admiralty Island National Monument: This area is essentially all wilderness except for the native village of Angoon. It is home to a large population of brown bears.

4. Tracy and Endicott arms: These arms lead back to glaciers, often visited by cruise ships.

5. Frederick Sound and Stephens Passage: Glacier ice is occasionally seen in this area that is popular among humpback whales.

6. Chatham Strait: Ruins of old canneries and whale, herring, and codfish plants are still found in many of the bays here. Salmon runs remain strong but refrigerated transport vessels take the fish to towns such as Petersburg for processing.

7. Point Baker: With its population of about 35, Point Baker is one of many roadless communities scattered throughout this island archipelago. Most residents are commercial fishers. Your mapmaker built a cabin here and wrote about his many adventures in his memoir, Alaska Blues.

8. Le Conte Bay: This is the most southerly place that a glacier reaches down to the saltwater. Off the beaten path, the rapidly retreating glacier calves its icebergs into a particularly beautiful bay.

9. Petersburg: Settled by Norwegian fishermen, today this town is the commercial fishing center of SE Alaska and has a bustling waterfront lined with canneries and fish freezer plants.

10. Wrangell Narrows: The narrows are a winding, 22-mile shortcut between Ketchikan and Juneau, widely used by small craft and Alaska state ferries. It is too narrow for big ships.

11. The Border Peaks: the U.S.-Canada border runs along the top of the highest peaks of the coastal range.

12. Stikine River: The river winds though the coastal mountains. It was an early gold-rush route to interior.

13. Prince of Wales Island: This is the fourth-largest island in the U.S. (after Kodiak, Hawaii, and Puerto Rico). During the heyday of logging in the 1960s, it was one of the wealthiest of Alaska zip codes. (Loggers are well paid.)

14. The Outside coast: There is only one town, Sitka, found on this very rough and remote 400-mile stretch of coast, seen in the map to right. Any lights you may see at night are apt to be anchored fishing boats.

15. Misty Fjords National Monument: This very rugged high country is penetrated by several deep and winding fjords. Excursions are available from Ketchikan to the most dramatic fjord, Rudyard Bay.

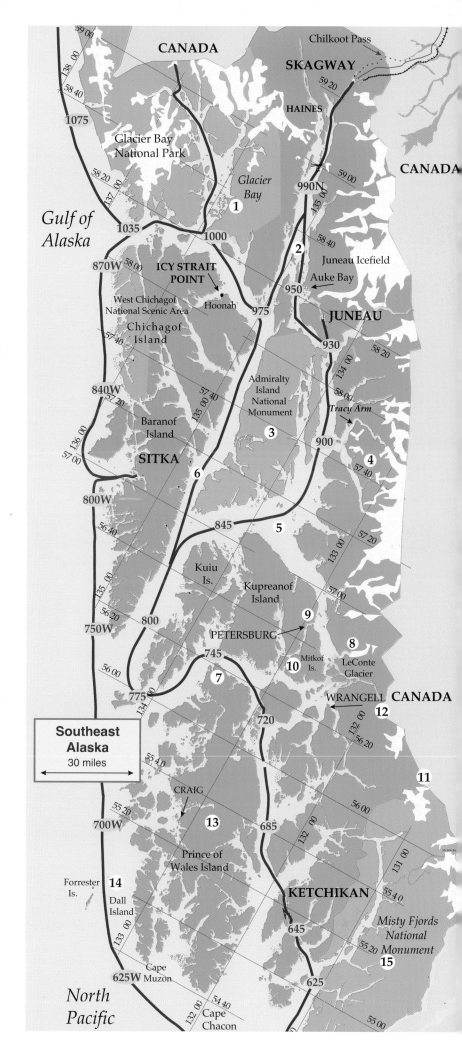

DISCOVERY of ALASKA

SEA COW
(AFTER WAXELL)

FUR SEAL

KAYAK I.

VOYAGE OF
1741
ALASKA FOUND!

ALEKSANDR
BARANOV

LORD OF ALASKA
1790 1818

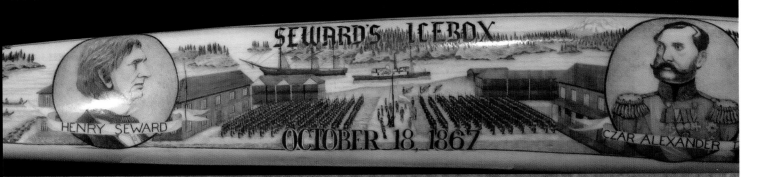

SEWARD'S ICEBOX

HENRY SEWARD

OCTOBER 18, 1867

CZAR ALEXANDER

KLONDIKE GOLD RUSH
1897-98

THE NOME NUGGET

NOME ALASKA SATURDAY JANUARY 24, 1925

DIPHTHERIA EPIDEMIC THREATENS

DEATH RACE BEGINS

ALASKA RAILROADS STEAM ENGINE 66 WITH
CHARLIE MATHIESON, ENGINEER, BEGAN
298 MILE RUN TO NENANA WITH ANTITOXIN
FOR NOME: WILD BILL SHANNON WITH DOG
TEAM WAITS IN -30° TEMPERATURE
NENANA

DOG TEAM STARTS
STRICKEN NOME WITH
ANTITOXIN SERUM

NENANA, JAN 28

SERUM RELAYED
BY TWENTY DO

NOME, FEB 2

TOGO NOT BALT
HERO SAYS L. SE
NOME, FEB 26

Alaska History Time Line

30,000 B.C.: Migratory hunters from Asia move across the land bridge from Siberia to Alaska, and settle North America.

8,000 B.C.: As the Ice Age ends, the rising ocean covers the land bridge. An ice bridge forms. Migration slows.

1741: Vitus Bering and Aleksei Chirikov land in Alaska on an expedition from Russia and take home 800 sea otter skins, but Bering is lost on the return. The fur traders begin outfitting new expeditions, and the fur rush is on.

1778: British Captain James Cook explores much of the Alaskan coast.

1792-4: British Captain George Vancouver exhaustively explores and charts the Northwest Coast with two ships.

1799: Alexander Baranov consolidates Russia's possession of Alaska with establishment of a fort and trading base at Sitka.

1867: Secretary of State William Seward buys Alaska from Czarist Russia for 2 cents an acre. Total purchase price: $7.2 million. By then, however, the fur resource has been depleted. The land deal is hailed as "Seward's Folly."

1879: Naturalist John Muir canoes throughout SE Alaska and discovers Glacier Bay. (When Captain Vancouver passed through, there was no bay to be seen, just ice.) Muir's reports inspire development of early tourism industry.

1896-1900: A gold strike on a Yukon River tributary attracts 100,000 people to the Yukon Territory and Alaska.

1922: Roy Jones makes the first float plane flight up the Inside Passage. It revolutionized bush travel in Alaska.

1925: A 674-mile dogsled relay brings diphtheria vaccine to Nome. The feat is celebrated today with the annual running of the Iditarod Trail Sled Dog Race from Anchorage to Nome.

1942: Japan invades the Aleutian Islands. The Alaska Highway project is begun to move defense supplies into the territory.

1959: Alaska becomes the 49th state.

1964: Good Friday earthquake kills 131 people in Alaska. It's a giant, the second-worst earthquake ever recorded.

1968: Ten billion barrels of oil are discovered at Prudhoe Bay.

1971: Congress settles Alaska Native land claims, conveying 40 million acres of land and $1 billion to the state's Natives.

1976: Federal 200-mile limit established around all US coastline, sets stage for major fisheries growth in Alaska .

1977: The first oil flows through the 800-mile trans-Alaska pipeline, a monumental engineering feat.

1980: Congress passes the Alaska National Interest Lands and Conservation Act (ANILCA), establishing millions of acres of federal park lands, wilderness areas, refuges, and other park units.

1989: The tanker *Exxon Valdez* rams a reef creating a massive oil spill and years of work for hundreds of lawyers.

2011 - US Supreme Court finally settles punitive damages to be paid by Exxon for spill.

Opposite page: Scenes from Alaska history are engraved on walrus tusks displayed at Dennis Corrington's Museum in his store in Skagway. Corrington was originally a school teacher who became an ivory-collector after seeing what some of his Native students' parents were carving.

Historical scenes, in descending order:

1. Russian Vitus Bering was probably the first European to set sight on Alaska. He died on the trip home, but some of his crew survived to bring the news of a fortune to be made with sea-otter furs.

2. Alexander Baranov ruled Russia's northwest empire that stretched all the way down to central California and was built on harvesting sea otters for their furs.

3. The formal transfer of Alaska from Russia took place at Sitka, and was derided as "Seward's Icebox."

4. The Klondike Gold Rush was the signal event that put Alaska on the map, even though almost all of it took place in Canada. Of the tens of thousands who left their homes to look for gold, only a few struck it rich.

5. A relay of dog teams ran over 500 miles to carry lifesaving diphtheria vaccine to Nome in 1925. Today that event is celebrated by the annual running of the Iditarod Trail Sled Dog Race, major winter event in Alaska.

Right: The happy beneficiary of one of Alaska's many resource booms. This man, Walter Kuhr, went from working as a crewman to operating numerous large crabbers and trawlers of his own. He was my crewmate on the crabber Flood Tide, in 1971.

The First People: An Enduring Culture

Wandering over the land bridge from Asia during the last ice age, spreading out among the islands of what is now SE Alaska, the First People learned that the sea and the forest provided. Eventually becoming primarily the Tlingit, Haida, and Tsimpshian, they endured the brutality of the Russians and new diseases to which they had no immunity, creating stable communities with time to create substantial art.

When the Russians sold Alaska to the US in 1867, both the seller and buyer seemed to have ignored the fact that a good deal of the vast region already belonged to the Natives.

The issue of Native land claims had to be settled before the Alaska oil pipeline could be built in the 1970s. Part of the $1 billion, 40-million-acre settlement created regional Native corporations, each of which received a substantial amount of money from the federal government. They invested in many things, including the Mount Roberts Tram in Juneau.

Yet, even after the settlement, much of the income in the Native villages of SE Alaska still comes from fishing and logging.

Photographs on these two pages were taken at Celebration 2010, the biannual Natives arts and culture festival held in Juneau. Natives from all around SE Alaska come to the capital to celebrate their heritage. The parade is a not-to–be-missed event.

Ketchikan: Before the big ships, it was fish and trees.

Twenty miles long and two blocks wide isn't a bad way to describe Ketchikan, spread along Tongass Narrows. Originally it was a rough–and-tumble fishing town, where Creek Street, the red-light district, was a busy busy place especially on the weekends when both fishermen and loggers came in to kick up their heels.

Then, after trying for years to find a way to market regional timber, the U.S. Forest Service finally facilitated construction of the big Ketchikan Pulp Mill in the early 1950s, and a sawmill operated on the docks where cruise ships tie up today. It was a welcome change from the earlier days when most jobs existed only during the salmon season, and everyone lived on credit during the long winters. In pulp mill days, logging was king, and many commercial fishermen felt like second-class citizens.

Unfortunately, driving bulldozers up salmon streams and clear-cutting whole valleys ridge to ridge reduced salmon catches and angered the commercial fishermen. Tougher logging regulations were established, and the mill closed in 1997.

Fortunately, salmon-fishing and processing is strong again. The cruise industry has created many seasonal jobs. Yet, without a large-year round employer like the old pulp mill, the 8,000 or so residents of Ketchikan still find that winter can be a lean and slow time economically after the big cruise ships stop coming.

Top: As much of residential Ketchikan is built on the hills over the water, its residents, many of whom are involved in the fishing business, get to watch all the activity around the waterfront right out their front windows!

Right: Ketchikan had its begining as a Native village and there are many new and old totem poles.

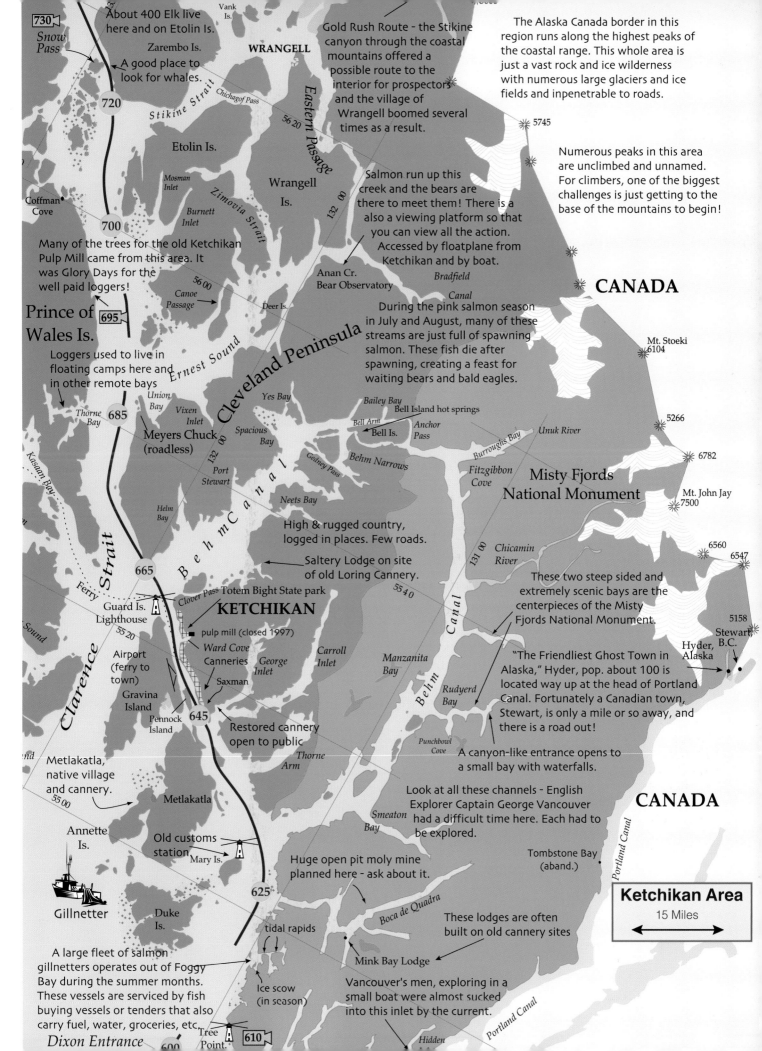

730

Snow Pass

About 400 Elk live here and on Etolin Is.

A good place to look for whales.

720

Zarembo Is.

Vank Is.

WRANGELL

Stikine Strait

Chichagof Pass

Etolin Is.

Mosman Inlet

Zimovia Strait

56 20

Eastern Passage

Gold Rush Route - the Stikine canyon through the coastal mountains offered a possible route to the interior for prospectors and the village of Wrangell boomed several times as a result.

The Alaska Canada border in this region runs along the highest peaks of the coastal range. This whole area is just a vast rock and ice wilderness with numerous large glaciers and ice fields and inpenetrable to roads.

Numerous peaks in this area are unclimbed and unnamed. For climbers, one of the biggest challenges is just getting to the base of the mountains to begin!

5745

Coffman Cove

700

Burnett Inlet

Wrangell Is.

56 00

Canoe Passage

Deer Is.

132 00

Salmon run up this creek and the bears are there to meet them! There is a also a viewing platform so that you can view all the action. Accessed by floatplane from Ketchikan and by boat.

Anan Cr. Bear Observatory

Bradfield

Canal

CANADA

Mt. Stoeki 6104

Many of the trees for the old Ketchikan Pulp Mill came from this area. It was Glory Days for the well paid loggers!

695

Prince of Wales Is.

Loggers used to live in floating camps here and in other remote bays

Ernest Sound

Union Bay

Vixen Inlet

Thorne Bay

685

Cleveland Peninsula

Yes Bay

Spacious Bay

Meyers Chuck (roadless)

132 00

Port Stewart

Helm Bay

Gedney Pass

Behm Narrows

During the pink salmon season in July and August, many of these streams are just full of spawning salmon. These fish die after spawning, creating a feast for waiting bears and bald eagles.

Bailey Bay

Bell Island hot springs

Bell Arm

Bell Is.

Anchor Pass

Burrough's Bay

Fitzgibbon Cove

Unuk River

5266

6782

Mt. John Jay 7500

Misty Fjords National Monument

6560

6547

Kasaan Bay

Clarence Strait

Ferry

665

Behm Canal

Neets Bay

High & rugged country, logged in places. Few roads.

Saltery Lodge on site of old Loring Cannery.

55 40

131 00

Chicamin River

These two steep sided and extremely scenic bays are the centerpieces of the Misty Fjords National Monument.

5158

Clover Pass Totem Bight State park

Guard Is. Lighthouse

Sound

55 20

KETCHIKAN

pulp mill (closed 1997)

Ward Cove Canneries

Airport (ferry to town)

Gravina Island

Pennock Island

Saxman

645

George Inlet

Carroll Inlet

Manzanita Bay

Behm Canal

Rudyerd Bay

Stewart, B.C.

Hyder, Alaska

"The Friendliest Ghost Town in Alaska," Hyder, pop. about 100 is located way up at the head of Portland Canal. Fortunately a Canadian town, Stewart, is only a mile or so away, and there is a road out!

Restored cannery open to public

Thorne Arm

Punchbowl Cove

A canyon-like entrance opens to a small bay with waterfalls.

Metlakatla, native village and cannery.

Metlakatla

Old customs station

Mary Is.

Annette Is.

Gillnetter

Duke Is.

625

Smeaton Bay

Look at all these channels - English Explorer Captain George Vancouver had a difficult time here. Each had to be explored.

Tombstone Bay (aband.)

CANADA

Portland Canal

Huge open pit moly mine planned here - ask about it.

Boca de Quadra

These lodges are often built on old cannery sites

Ketchikan Area
15 Miles

A large fleet of salmon gillnetters operates out of Foggy Bay during the summer months. These vessels are serviced by fish buying vessels or tenders that also carry fuel, water, groceries, etc.

tidal rapids

Ice scow (in season)

Mink Bay Lodge

Vancouver's men, exploring in a small boat were almost sucked into this inlet by the current.

Tree Point

610

600

Dixon Entrance

Hidden

Portland Canal

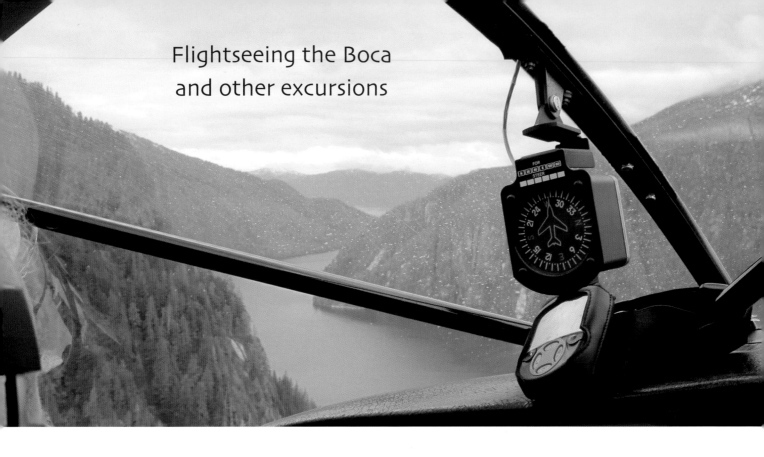

Flightseeing the Boca
and other excursions

Ketchikan Excursions: (change seasonally)

Misty Fjords—by air or sea, or a combination
Bering Sea Fishermen's Tour on a crab boat
Coastal Wildlife Cruise
Wilderness Exploration and Crab Feast
Sea Kayaking
Rainforest Wildlife Sanctuary Hike
Neets Bay Bear Watch and Seaplane Flight
Rainforest Ropes Course and Zip-line Park
Bear Creek Zip-line
Adventure Kart Expedition
Back Country Hummer Expedition—U Drive
Flightseeing and Crab Feast
Totem Bight Park and Town Tour
Totem Bight and Lumberjack Show Combo
Saxman Native Village tour
Town and Harbor Duck Tour
Motorcycle Tour—U Drive
Sports-fishing Expedition
Sports-fishing & Wilderness Dining
Alaskan Chef's Table
City Highlights Trolley Tour
Mountain Point Snorkeling Adventure
And, as they say, many more...

Top: Flight-seeing plane entering Misty Fjords.
Tours by fast boat are also available.
Right, middle: Logging show in downtown Ketchikan
celebrates woods work.
Right, bottom: Carver Nathan Jackson at work in the
carving shed at Saxman.

Bear Country

When the salmon run in Alaska, first they travel up streams to their spawning grounds, then after the female lays and the male fertilizes the eggs, both fish die. Their remains comprise a major part of the yearly diet of both black and brown bears and eagles.

The largest population of bears in SE Alaska are black, up to perhaps 600 pounds. Most brown or grizzly bears live in western Alaska, though there are populations on Admiralty Island and in scattered coastal locations. "Brownies" are huge. The males weight as much as a ton!

Top and lower left: Bears at Anan Creek north of Ketchikan. Don't think you can escape a bear by climbing a tree.

Left-middle and above: Brown bears (identified by the hump on their shoulders) in the Brooks Falls area of the Katmai National Park west of Anchorage.

Commercial Fishing

Fortunately, unlike Canada's, Alaska's fishery resources have been well managed and are generally strong. Refrigerated fish-transport vessels, called "tenders" or "packers," bring in fish from remote areas to processing in the towns.

Commercial fishing is tightly regulated by area, gear type, and fishing time. The return of salmon to streams is carefully monitored and fishing time tailored to make sure enough salmon return to spawn to create the next generation.

In recent years, processors have moved to build facilities to freeze more of their salmon instead of canning it, creating a higher-value product. Salmon roe, for export to Japan, has evolved to be a premium product.

Many young men and women who put themselves through college by working on salmon boats have discovered that fishing makes for a great job after college as well. In the recent big years, many of the crews on good purse seiners, such as the one above, made close to $50,000 for the three-month season while crew shares on top boats might double that!

Top: The crew of a salmon purse-seiner, deeply loaded with fish, hauls the last of a set or haul aboard. DK

Left: Your author's crew watches a group of salmon hit and struggle in his gillnet.

Top: A single-handed salmon troller working the big waters of Veda Bay, Noyes Island. More than any other fishery, trolling is often a solitary pursuit, with just a single person on surprisingly large vessels like this one.

Above: Petersburg cannery worker celebrating his Norwegian heritage as he loads valuable salmon roe onto a pallet for export.

Right: A crew member aboard a salmon troller displays a healthy-looking king salmon. DK

Along The Way: Ketchikan to Juneau

Top: Floating home, Coffman Cove, **Mile 700**. *With good fishing in near-by Clarence Strait, this gillnetting family wanted to live close by, but there was no land for sale. So, in an example of true Alaskan ingenuity, they first built a raft out of huge beachcombed logs. Then, with a small portable sawmill, they cut boards for a deck over the raft, and finally built a home and a shop on the raft. Years later, when land in the cove became available, they purchased a lot, beached the raft at high tide, and hired a bulldozer to tow their home to their new lot overlooking the cove where their floating home used to be.*

Above: Breaching humpback, near **Mile 870**. *It's not clear why whales do this—perhaps to dislodge parasites? But breaching is spectacular, and fairly common—keep your eyes peeled. Alaskastock*

Right: Sea lions at a rookery near Tracy Arm. The big guy is a bull, who might weigh a ton or more. He would often live with a "harem" and guard them jealously.

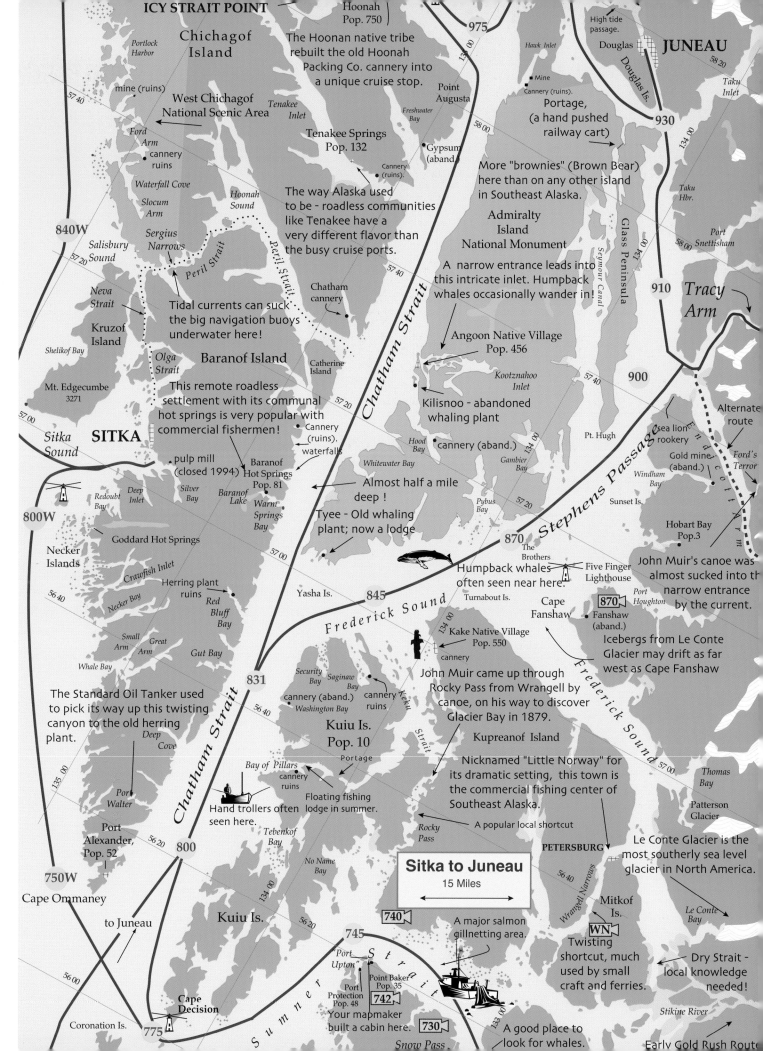

ICY STRAIT POINT

Chichagof Island

Portlock Harbor

mine (ruins)

West Chichagof National Scenic Area

Ford Arm
cannery ruins

Waterfall Cove

Slocum Arm

Hoonah Sound

Sergius Narrows

Salisbury Sound

840W   57 20

Neva Strait

Kruzof Island

Shelikof Bay

Olga Strait

Mt. Edgecumbe 3271

57 00

Sitka Sound

SITKA

800W

Redoubt Bay

Deep Inlet

Silver Bay

Necker Islands

Goddard Hot Springs

Crawfish Inlet

56 40

Necker Bay

Herring plant ruins

Red Bluff Bay

Small Arm   *Great Arm*

Gut Bay

Whale Bay

The Standard Oil Tanker used to pick its way up this twisting canyon to the old herring plant.

Deep Cove

135 00

Port Walter

Port Alexander, Pop. 52

56 20

750W

Cape Ommaney

to Juneau

Kuiu Is.

56 00

Hoonah Pop. 750

The Hoonan native tribe rebuilt the old Hoonah Packing Co. cannery into a unique cruise stop.

Tenakee Inlet

Point Augusta

Freshwater Bay

Tenakee Springs Pop. 132

Gypsum (aband.)

Cannery (ruins).

975

High tide passage.

Douglas   **JUNEAU**

Hawk Inlet   58 20

Mine

Cannery (ruins).

Portage, (a hand pushed railway cart)

Douglas Is.

930

58 00

134 00

Taku Inlet

Taku Hbr.

Port Snettisham

The way Alaska used to be - roadless communities like Tenakee have a very different flavor than the busy cruise ports.

Hoonah Sound

57 40

Tidal currents can suck the big navigation buoys underwater here!

Chatham cannery

Baranof Island

This remote roadless settlement with its communal hot springs is very popular with commercial fishermen!

pulp mill (closed 1994)

Baranof Hot Springs Pop. 81

Baranof Lake

Warm Springs Bay

Cannery (ruins). waterfalls

Almost half a mile deep !

Tyee - Old whaling plant; now a lodge

Chatham Strait

57 20

Catherine Island

Whitewater Bay

Hood Bay

cannery (aband.)

57 00

845

Yasha Is.

More "brownies" (Brown Bear) here than on any other island in Southeast Alaska.

Admiralty Island National Monument

A narrow entrance leads into this intricate inlet. Humpback whales occasionally wander in!

Angoon Native Village Pop. 456

Kootznahoo Inlet

Kilisnoo - abandoned whaling plant

Pt. Hugh

Gambier Bay

Pybus Bay

134 00

57 20

870

The Brothers

Seymour Canal

Glass Peninsula

134 00

57 40

900

910

Tracy Arm

Endicott Arm

Alternate route

Ford's Terror

sea lion rookery

Gold mine (aband.)

Windham Bay

Sunset Is.

Hobart Bay Pop.3

John Muir's canoe was almost sucked into the narrow entrance by the current.

Icebergs from Le Conte Glacier may drift as far west as Cape Fanshaw

Stephens Passage

Five Finger Lighthouse

Port Houghton

870

Cape Fanshaw

Fanshaw (aband.)

Frederick Sound

Humpback whales often seen near here.

Frederick Sound

Turnabout Is.

134 00

Kake Native Village Pop. 550

cannery

John Muir came up through Rocky Pass from Wrangell by canoe, on his way to discover Glacier Bay in 1879.

Kuiu Is. Pop. 10

Security Bay   *Saginaw Bay*

cannery (aband.)   cannery ruins

Washington Bay

Keku Strait

Kupreanof Island

Nicknamed "Little Norway" for its dramatic setting, this town is the commercial fishing center of Southeast Alaska.

A popular local shortcut

PETERSBURG

Thomas Bay

Patterson Glacier

Le Conte Glacier is the most southerly sea level glacier in North America.

831

Chatham Strait

56 40

The Standard Oil Tanker used to pick its way up this twisting canyon...

Portage

Bay of Pillars
cannery ruins

Floating fishing lodge in summer.

Hand trollers often seen here.

Tebenkof Bay

56 20

No Name Bay

Rocky Pass

Wrangell Narrows

Mitkof Is.

56 40

WN

Twisting shortcut, much used by small craft and ferries.

Le Conte Bay

Dry Strait - local knowledge needed!

800

Kuiu Is.

56 20

Cape Decision

Coronation Is.

775

Sitka to Juneau
15 Miles

740

745

"Port Upton"

Port Protection Pop. 48

Point Baker Pop. 35

742

Your mapmaker built a cabin here.

730

Snow Pass

Sumner Strait

A major salmon gillnetting area.

A good place to look for whales.

Stikine River

Early Gold Rush Route

An Alaska Retirement

At Point Baker, in the 1970s, my neighbor was Old Flea. He had his little boat, a cozy cabin, and his social security check. The fish buyer was also our bartender, and after selling his fish, Flea would get a six pack for the skiff ride home.

When newcomers came to town, he'd show them the ropes, the best places to fish, help them get started. And until they got on their feet, give them his fish money.

Not a bad retirement.

When we built our waterfront cabin near roadless Point Baker, Mile 742, in the 1970s, our new home came with an unexpected bonus: a bunch of humpbacks as our nearest neighbors.

It turned out that there was a tidal eddy in Sumner Strait right in front of our cabin that often would push herring into balls, or small schools. One humpback, nicknamed Ma Baker, and sometimes her companion, would hang out there all summer chowing down on the fish.

Once my parents were visiting and wanted to catch a salmon. I had boatwork to do, so I sent them out in my skiff and told them there was pretty good fishing right out front.

So off they went to catch a nice salmon for supper. A while later, I heard what sounded like excited voices and figured they had just landed a nice one. But when they got back in, I found out it was a different story.

"The engine stopped," my dad said, "I couldn't get it started; then, these two whales came. They were so close we could smell their breath. We were terrified!"

Top: Whales are pretty social, often traveling in groups to help each other herd herring into schools for easier eating. AS

Right, middle: Two humpbacks right in front of our cove.

Right, bottom: Local lore had it that once Ma Baker surfaced under one of the local skiffs, lifting it clear of the water, but without capsizing it! DK

Noyes Island: Fishing on The Edge

April 30, 1973: Gray and cold with engines starting on all sides at 5 a.m. Wind howling in the rigging all night; should have slept in, but the big boys headed out, so put on two wool shirts, screwed up our courage and followed. Passed Cape Ulitka, a dirty spot where the ocean pours around the point, and almost turned around right there.

The swells on the outside were 15 feet high, mean and ominous in the early morning light with a wind chop on top. Ran out to the 30-fathom line and went back in the stern to start setting out our lines to troll for salmon. A mile and a half away loomed the dark wall of Noyes Island, clouds low on the hills and the shores lost in the spume of the breaking seas. They call this the Gulf of Alaska, but it's really the North Pacific Ocean, and the shores show the effects of the winter gales that have scraped off all the vegetation up to a hundred feet above the water.

Just a handful of fish and weather deteriorating all the time, so I fished with an eye over my shoulder. But still, once a big one surprised us and filled the stern.

If you only see Cape Addington once, it should be on such a day as this. The wind was coming on hard and running against the tide, and the cape, a long rocky arm, was almost lost in the mists as heavy seas beat against its rocky sides. That's an evil place, and we gave it plenty of room in order to stay clear of the tide rips, but even so it was a wild hour before we got past. Once, on top of a big one, I looked around. To the south the water was white and the sky dark. A quarter-mile away, a single boat labored through the tide rip, but otherwise we were alone.

Then it was an hour's run through the big swells at Cone Island and finally into the shelter of a protected cove. Crew rowed ashore to walk the dog, and I poured a stiff one and went to sort out the mess on the back deck. Seven king salmon for the day."

Top: A seine skiff operator tows the end of a salmon purse seine net as close as he dares to the shore near Cape Addington. The job of the "skiff man" calls for good nerves. Sometimes you have to work on the very edge of the breakers. Duncan Kowalski

Above: A salmon troller half hidden by the swells off Noyes Island. Fishing for king salmon is often good here in April and May, but as you can see, it is certainly fishing for the hardy. At that time of year, it sometimes blows so hard that you have to lay on your anchor two days for every day of fishing.

The Handloggers: Big Men and Bigger Trees

Top: Drawing by Christine Cox depicts handloggers working on a springboard high above an inlet in northern British Columbia. Inset map shows typical fjord country preferred by handloggers.

Above: Handloggers. Legendary Alaska handlogger W.H. Jackson said he almost hit a float plane once with a big tree he was taking down. UW 12141

Before the arrival of floating logging camps and the chainsaws and skidders of today's industrial logging, there were a few men, rowing or motoring up and down the coast in small boats, looking for the biggest trees on the steepest slopes.

Like the legendary Douglas fir that was 300 feet tall and 15 feet in diameter. Or the spruce that contained 22,000 board feet of lumber that handloggers towed to the old mill at Swanson Bay, **Mile 462.**

The trick was to find a bay with extra steep slopes. Then, climbing up with your double-bitted axe and iron-tipped springboard, you'd look for a big tree that could be cut in such a way that it would either fall directly into the water or slide all the way down into the water. Then walking along those floating giants, the handlogger would lop off the branches until he had a single huge log.

If you were good, or lucky, that's what would happen—the tree would make it all the way to the water without help. If it didn't (even on the steepest slopes, a tree could hit another tree or a rock and get stuck), that's when the hard work began. The handlogger would have to get out a heavy jack to lift the stuck end up to get it sliding again. This could be more dangerous than the actual cutting because on steep slopes, a big tree could take off in a rush after just a slight push, and the handlogger would have to scramble to get out of the way.

Sometimes a big, big tree might take several days to get down into the water, especially if it hung up on the way down. Log by log, a raft would be assembled. And then the handlogger would row or get word to the mill to send a tug for the logs. Only then, when the logs had been delivered to the mill, would the handlogger be paid.

51

Filming Stories at Le Conte Bay

Off the beaten path, hidden in the coastal mountains east of Petersburg, is Le Conte Bay. It's a stunning spot—one of Alaska's secret places—but with unpredictable, rapidly changing weather and swiftly flowing tides. The bay presented challenging conditions for film-maker Dan Kowalski and me.

But we found a place on the beach to set up video cameras and audio recorder. At the edge of the place where we were filming was a small beached iceberg, about the size of a dump truck. I was thinking of going over and leaning against it. Before I could do it, the iceberg suddenly collapsed with big chunks crashing onto the very place I would have been standing.

I was lucky that day. It was a reminder that the wilderness is always waiting—for the foolish, for the careless, and or just the unlucky.

We shot until the rising tide made us move. Next, we tried a long shot with Dan on his boat anchored in a cove, and me on shore with a ra-dio microphone, talking about Le Conte.

In the early evening, after the tide eased, we anchored away from the ice, and climbed into the skiff to go out among the big bergs.

We let the sun get a little lower, find some

Top: Dan filming me with a Nikon D7000. I was talking about Le Conte, while we drifted slowly among the ice. Left top: Shooting on the beach at low tide.

Left bottom: While only sticking up about 8' from the water, the underwater part of this berg is about the size of a two car garage. DK

clouds to diffuse it, and suddenly we had that moment with the perfect soft light that filmmakers wait for.

We turned the motor off, and I let the currents push us in a slow circle among the bergs while I talked and Dan filmed. It was perfect.

We shot until dusk, then it was time to pick our way through the bergs in the failing light and get across lower Frederick Sound to a safe anchorage. It was black before we got clear, and I was cooking with just a dimmed headlamp so as not to disturb Dan's night vision, least he T-bone one of the floating pieces of ice, which by then were essentially invisible.

In the foggy black, guided only by the eerie pale shapes on our radar screen and plotter, we found a safe anchorage in the protection of a dot of an island, dropped the anchor, and shut everything down to savor the welcome silence.

When it was coffee time the next morning, we looked out at such a lovely and peaceful sight: the few acres of island just emerging from the dawn sun-lit fog, with seals popping up curiously around us, and the cry of crows and ravens in the trees.

Top: Dan on the fly bridge with his coffee. We should have started up and gotten underway sooner, but the spot was so special we didn't want to spoil it with engine noise.

Right, middle: Picking our way among the icebergs at dusk trying to find an anchorage where the ice wouldn't whack us in the middle of the night. As it got full dark, the bergs seemed to have this luminous light from the half-moon flitting through the clouds.

Right, bottom: Dan checks "takes" on a laptop computer on his bunk.

The Small Ship Experience

Small ships offer a much more intimate experience than large ones. This is the *Wilderness Adventurer*, carrying about 50 passengers on a week-long cruise between Ketchikan and Juneau.

Typically such cruises will concentrate less on the ports than anchoring up and exploring places where passengers may hike and kayak, usually with no one else in sight. For information: Uncruises.com

Top: Getting into your kayak is easy.
Above: Kayaking instructions.
Left, below: Your mapmaker and wife, Mary Lou.
Left, middle: Hikers hit the beach in Thomas Bay.
Opposite page: Exploring Fords Terror and Endicott Arm

THAN OF THE DEEP

Exploring Lonely Chatham Strait

For much of the last century, Chatham Strait was a beehive of activity. Between the salmon plants, herring plants, and whaling stations, almost every bay in this canyon-like region was home to some sort of commercial activity, frenzied during the summer fishing season and sleepy in winter, with just a watchman.

Then, the herring and the whales disappeared, and refrigerated tenders allowed consolidation of the salmon canneries into towns like Petersburg and Ketchikan.

For the small-craft traveler today, it is almost spooky to travel in Chatham Strait, to anchor and go ashore and wander among the ruins, rarely encountering another traveler.

One of the few settlements along here is Port Alexander, **Mile 792**. With a good harbor, a settlement, a fish-buyer and a store, plus good fishing at Cape Ommaney (west of **Mile 786**), it's a popular spot in summer. In its heyday, it was Alaska with a capital A, as an old-timer noted: "It became the—number one trolling port in the territory, a wide-open, carefree, money-kissed little place…"

Top: Sperm whale at the Port Armstrong plant, circa 1910. MOHAI 15329
Left, middle: Troller exiting from Big Port Walter
Left, bottom: In an abandoned cabin, a Victrola waits for owners who will never return.
Opposite: small cruise ship in Endicott Arm

Tracy and Endicott Arms

Tracy Arm, a winding fjord close to Juneau, is both an alternate stop for ships unable to get a permit to visit Glacier Bay and a destination for Juneau-based excursions.

Many ships enter Tracy Arm early in order to make a port stop in Juneau later the same day. **Tip**: If yours has a schedule like this, be sure to get up in time to see the entrance, and in particular the dramatic right-angle turn.

Also, look for glacial striations along the sides of the fjord. These are long scars or gouges parallel to the water that were created when rocks embedded in the glacier were carried with it as it moved down from the snow fields in the mountains, grinding grooves into the fjord walls.

Occasionally, because of fog or too much ice in Tracy Arm, ships will visit Endicott Arm to the south instead and get as close to the ice at Dawes Glacier as they can. Don't be disappointed: It is almost as dramatic as Tracy Arm; just a little farther from Juneau.

Top: What's wrong with this photo? (Except for no lifejackets.. we were way too casual back then...) Actually, getting this close to a big iceberg like this is very risky. 7/8th of an iceberg is underwater, and melting faster than the part exposed to air, often causes the iceberg to roll over without warning, creating waves small enough to capsize small craft like this..

Left: passengers from a small ship explore the steep shore of Tracy Arm.

This bend is very dramatic in early morning light.

Tracy Arm

← 5 miles →

North Sawyer Glacier

South Sawyer Glacier

900

Top: Kayakers from a small ship in front of Dawes Glacier, Endicott Arm. The telephoto lens makes them seem dangerously close; actually, they are about a half-mile off, about as close as you would want to get in a kayak, least a big berg calve, creating a wave that could easily capsize you.

Above: Entering Tracy Arm

Right: This iceberg in Fords Terror split in half and almost rolled onto our small boat while we were photographing it. It was a near miss and reminded me once again not to get too close to bergs.

Hiking a Receding Glacier

An hour from their drop-off point, 16 miles north of Petersburg, hikers from a small cruise ship finally get to the top of Baird glacier. Receding glaciers sometimes change radically as they melt. The previous year, a large melt-water pool completely blocked the hikers' route. In 2013, visitors were lucky; the pool had shrunk, and they could hike around it.

Juneau

A bear? Behind the espresso stand? No roads in or out? You have to travel by boat or plane? What kind of a state capital is this?

Almost surrounded by high mountains and with a vast ice field—larger than Rhode Island—to the north, Juneau winters are substantially colder than that of Ketchikan or Sitka. Tlingit natives had fish camps near where downtown is today, but wintered in a more temperate and sheltered area near Auke Bay.

Alaska's first gold rush started here in 1880, but after the easy-to-find streambed gold was gathered quickly, industrial-scale, deep tunnel mining was needed to follow the veins deep underground. Massive stamp mills were built to extract gold; it wasn't uncommon for 20 or more tons of ore to be dug and processed to yield a single ounce of fine gold. The tailings—the crushed rock that was left—were dumped along the shore, creating the flat land on which today's downtown Juneau was built.

At peak capacity, the big stamp mills of the Alaska-Juneau mine, still visible above the cruise-ship docks, could crush 12,000 tons of ore a day. Working conditions were dangerous. The entrance to the big Treadwell mine was nicknamed the "glory Hole," for all the miners—sometimes one a week—that went to glory there. Eventually the gold played out, the tunnels—by then down to 2100 feet below the channel—filled with water, and today all that's left are ruins and miles of tunnels.

Top: Turbo Otters waiting for customers, downtown Juneau.
Right: View from the top of the Mount Roberts Tram. The water in the distance is Auke Bay and Lynn Canal. Glacier Bay lies on the other side of the far mountains.

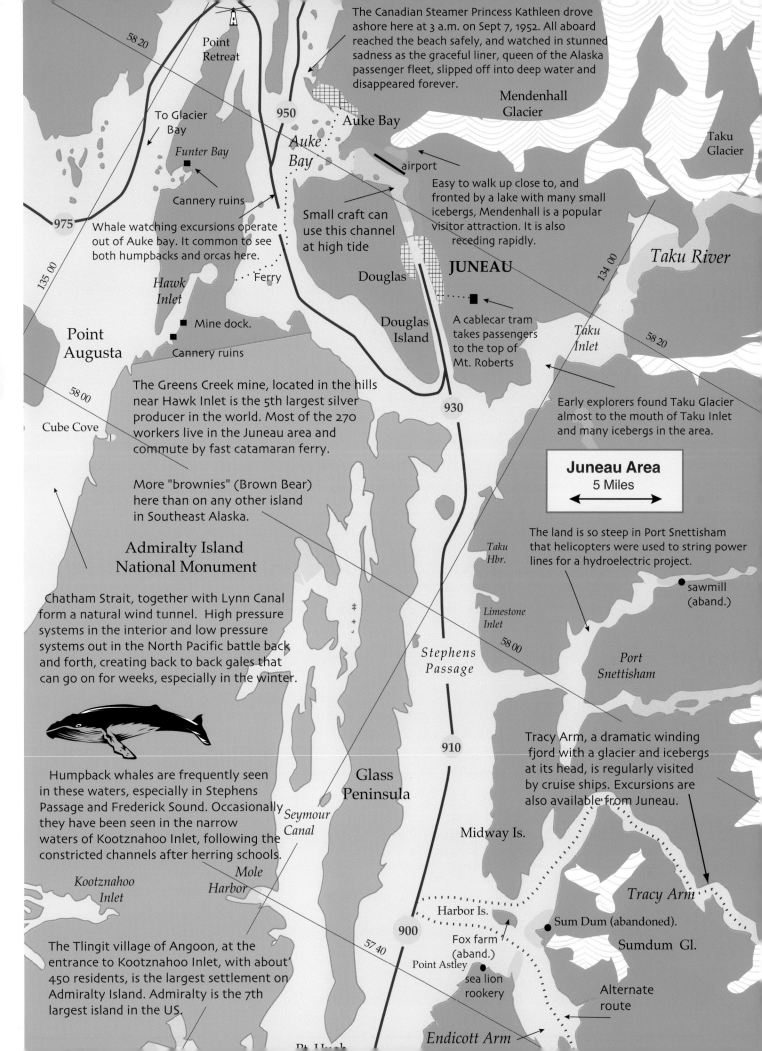

The Canadian Steamer Princess Kathleen drove ashore here at 3 a.m. on Sept 7, 1952. All aboard reached the beach safely, and watched in stunned sadness as the graceful liner, queen of the Alaska passenger fleet, slipped off into deep water and disappeared forever.

58 20

Point Retreat

950

To Glacier Bay

Funter Bay

Auke Bay

Mendenhall Glacier

Taku Glacier

975

Cannery ruins

Whale watching excursions operate out of Auke bay. It common to see both humpbacks and orcas here.

135 00

Hawk Inlet

Ferry

Small craft can use this channel at high tide

Douglas

airport

Easy to walk up close to, and fronted by a lake with many small icebergs, Mendenhall is a popular visitor attraction. It is also receding rapidly.

Taku River

JUNEAU

134 00

Point Augusta

Mine dock.

Cannery ruins

Douglas Island

58 20

Taku Inlet

A cablecar tram takes passengers to the top of Mt. Roberts

930

58 00

Cube Cove

The Greens Creek mine, located in the hills near Hawk Inlet is the 5th largest silver producer in the world. Most of the 270 workers live in the Juneau area and commute by fast catamaran ferry.

More "brownies" (Brown Bear) here than on any other island in Southeast Alaska.

Early explorers found Taku Glacier almost to the mouth of Taku Inlet and many icebergs in the area.

Juneau Area
5 Miles
⟷

Admiralty Island National Monument

Chatham Strait, together with Lynn Canal form a natural wind tunnel. High pressure systems in the interior and low pressure systems out in the North Pacific battle back and forth, creating back to back gales that can go on for weeks, especially in the winter.

Taku Hbr.

The land is so steep in Port Snettisham that helicopters were used to string power lines for a hydroelectric project.

• sawmill (aband.)

Limestone Inlet

58 00

Stephens Passage

Port Snettisham

Humpback whales are frequently seen in these waters, especially in Stephens Passage and Frederick Sound. Occasionally they have been seen in the narrow waters of Kootznahoo Inlet, following the constricted channels after herring schools.

Seymour Canal

910

Glass Peninsula

Midway Is.

Tracy Arm, a dramatic winding fjord with a glacier and icebergs at its head, is regularly visited by cruise ships. Excursions are also available from Juneau.

Kootznahoo Inlet

Mole Harbor

Harbor Is.

Tracy Arm

The Tlingit village of Angoon, at the entrance to Kootznahoo Inlet, with about 450 residents, is the largest settlement on Admiralty Island. Admiralty is the 7th largest island in the US.

57 40

900

Fox farm (aband.)

Point Astley

sea lion rookery

Sum Dum (abandoned).

Sumdum Gl.

Alternate route

Endicott Arm

Pt. Hugh

Juneau Excursions

Juneau Excursions
(Subject to seasonal changes)

Mendenhall Glacier Explorer
Mendenhall Gl. & Salmon Hatchery Tour
Original Alaska Salmon Bake
Underground Juneau
Rainforest Garden
A Taste of Juneau
Guide's Choice Adventure Hike
Dog Sled Summer Camp
Gold Panning & History Tour
Glacier View Bike & Brew
Rainforest Canopy & Zip-line Expedition
Mountain Zip & Rainforest Bike Ride
Juneau Sport-fishing Adventure
Juneau Steamboat Cruise
Photo Safari by Land & Sea
Alaska's Whales & Rainforest Trails
Whale Watching & Wildlife Quest
Mendenhall Glacier & Whale Quest
Whale Watching & Orca Point Lodge
Mendenhall Glacier Float Trip
Glacier View Sea Kayaking
Mendenhall Glacier Canoe Adventure
Taku Glacier Lodge Flight & Feast
Pilot's Choice Ice Age Exploration
Mendenhall Glacier Helicopter Tour
Four Glacier Adventure by Helicopter
Glacier & Dog Sled Adventure by Helicopter
Dog Sledding on the Mendenhall
Custom Hummer Adventure

Left top: Zipline on Douglas Island.
Left bottom: Captain John George offers steam-boat tours.

Around Town

Top: How'd you like to climb these stairs with your groceries on a snowy, dark evening? Many houses and cabins are accessed only by steep stairs. A good walk is the Flume Trail accessed via Basin Road off of 8th Avenue.

Above: Gold-panning

Right: Marchers at Celebration, the biannual Native festival in downtown Juneau in August, 2010. Tribes from all over SE Alaska gather to celebrate their culture. The highlights are performances by Native dancers and the parade.

Skagway

It is the drama of 1897 and '98 that fills this town. Skagway blossomed for few years, lawless and rough, and then almost disappeared. Yet, surprisingly, it survived. Today, the town still retains its charm and the ghosts of the men who passed through in the epic Klondike Gold Rush still walk these streets.

Those gaunt-faced men have passed through to whatever fate The North had in store for them. But the town the boom built at the jumping-off place for the Klondike remains, historically important and looking much as it did then, when some 80 saloons and many professional women served the lonely men on their way north.

Skagway was essentially built between 1897 and 1900. It was the weather that kept the turn of the 20th Century buildings intact. Buildings that would have rotted away without maintenance in rainy Ketchikan, endured longer in this much drier, sunnier climate.

Today, Skagway offers a unique experience to visitors. Even the vegetation and climate is different from the rest of SE Alaska because the town is under the influence of the harsher temperature extremes of the interior instead of the milder, cloudier maritime climate elsewhere in the region.

Skagway can get very busy. It is a not-to-be-missed town, but if you are a repeat passenger and are ready for something a little quieter, a fast ferry (45 minutes, $68 round-trip) can take you to Haines and historic Port Chilkoot, where there are some pleasant walks, a few galleries, and restaurants overlooking Lynn Canal.

Top: Downtown Skagway is quiet at dinnertime, when most passengers are eating aboard their ships. On a "four-ship day," 8,000 or more visitors hit the streets of this town that has a winter population of 900 souls.

Right: The train comes right to the ships in Skagway, making it convenient to take an excellent rail excursion. Built too late to accommodate most of those headed to the Gold Rush, the White Pass & Yukon Route survived on transporting Canadian ore but eventually ceased operations—until tourism brought the railroad back to life.

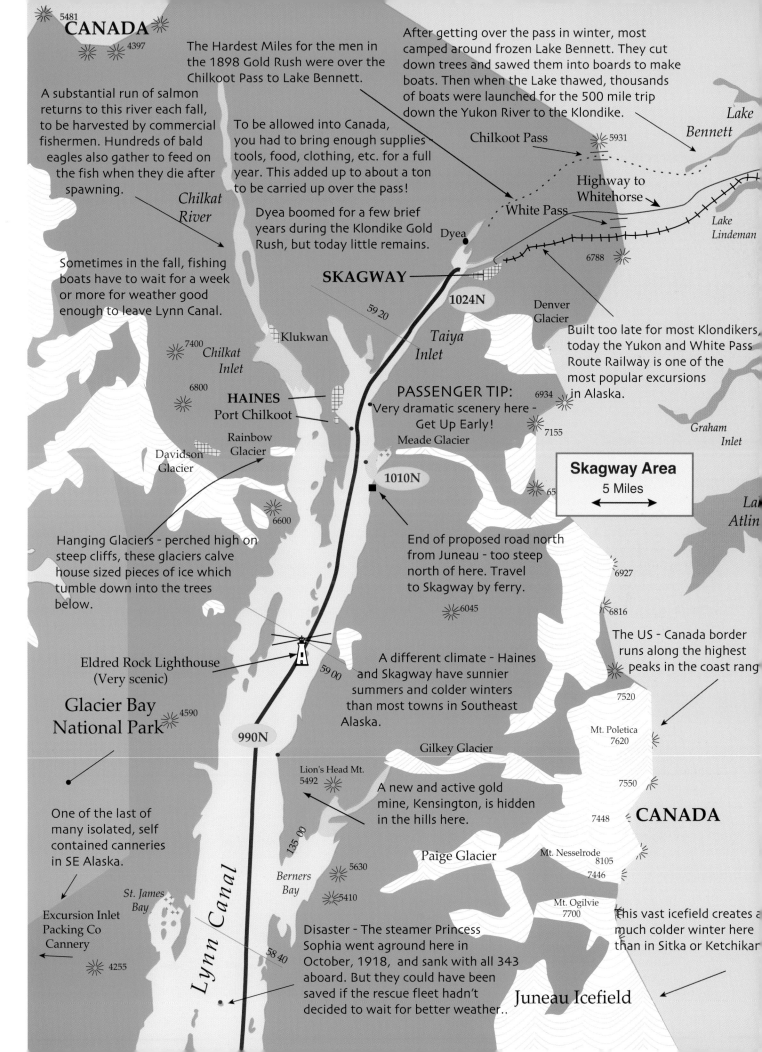

CANADA
5481
4397

The Hardest Miles for the men in the 1898 Gold Rush were over the Chilkoot Pass to Lake Bennett.

After getting over the pass in winter, most camped around frozen Lake Bennett. They cut down trees and sawed them into boards to make boats. Then when the Lake thawed, thousands of boats were launched for the 500 mile trip down the Yukon River to the Klondike.

A substantial run of salmon returns to this river each fall, to be harvested by commercial fishermen. Hundreds of bald eagles also gather to feed on the fish when they die after spawning.

To be allowed into Canada, you had to bring enough supplies tools, food, clothing, etc. for a full year. This added up to about a ton to be carried up over the pass!

Lake Bennett

Chilkoot Pass
5931

Highway to Whitehorse

White Pass

Lake Lindeman

Chilkat River

Dyea boomed for a few brief years during the Klondike Gold Rush, but today little remains.

Dyea

Sometimes in the fall, fishing boats have to wait for a week or more for weather good enough to leave Lynn Canal.

SKAGWAY

1024N

59 20

Taiya Inlet

6788

Denver Glacier

Built too late for most Klondikers, today the Yukon and White Pass Route Railway is one of the most popular excursions in Alaska.

Klukwan

7400 *Chilkat Inlet*

6800

HAINES
Port Chilkoot

PASSENGER TIP:
Very dramatic scenery here - Get Up Early!
Meade Glacier

6934

7155

Graham Inlet

Rainbow Glacier

Davidson Glacier

1010N

Skagway Area
5 Miles

La Atlin

6600

End of proposed road north from Juneau - too steep north of here. Travel to Skagway by ferry.

65

Hanging Glaciers - perched high on steep cliffs, these glaciers calve house sized pieces of ice which tumble down into the trees below.

6927

6816

Eldred Rock Lighthouse (Very scenic)

6045

The US - Canada border runs along the highest peaks in the coast rang

Glacier Bay National Park 4590

990N

A different climate - Haines and Skagway have sunnier summers and colder winters than most towns in Southeast Alaska.

Gilkey Glacier

7520

Mt. Poletica 7620

Lion's Head Mt. 5492

A new and active gold mine, Kensington, is hidden in the hills here.

7550

One of the last of many isolated, self contained canneries in SE Alaska.

Paige Glacier

Mt. Nesselrode 8105

7446

7448 **CANADA**

St. James Bay

59 00

135 00

Berners Bay 5630

5410

Mt. Ogilvie 7700

This vast icefield creates a much colder winter here than in Sitka or Ketchikan

Excursion Inlet Packing Co Cannery

4255

Lynn Canal

58 40

Disaster - The steamer Princess Sophia went aground here in October, 1918, and sank with all 343 aboard. But they could have been saved if the rescue fleet hadn't decided to wait for better weather..

Juneau Icefield

P ick up a copy of the walking tour map at the AB Hall. It's got directions up to the Gold Rush Cemetery, the Trail of '98 Museum, and other points of interest. It's definitely worthwhile to walk around with the map as your guide.

Of course, Skagway's signature hike is up the old Chilkoot Trail. This is way, way more than a pleasant stroll; more like a grueling four- to five-day epic, and that's in summer, not in the depth of winter with the poorly insulated clothing of the day and 2,000 pounds of gear to pack over the summit. If you start up the trail, think about this: Many of the men who used the trail made a dozen or more trips back and forth to ferry their loads or hired a Native porter.

Dyea was the start of the Chilkoot Trail. Not much is left now; Skagway boomed, Dyea died. Though Klondikers came ashore at Dyea; today the town is far from the water, due to glacial rebound. This occurs for centuries after glaciers have receded: the land, no longer carrying the immense weight of a glacier, slowly rises up. Even though the rise at Dyea is only about three-quarters of an inch a year, in the 114 years since the Gold Rush, the land has risen seven feet, enough to push the waterfront a good quarter-mile back.

Top: The Skagway Streetcar Tour is a good way to see town.

Right: Entrepreneur Dennis Corrington shows one of the excellent masks in his gift shop on Main Street. Don't miss his museum.

Opposite page, top: The challenges of The North were just too much for many who made it no farther than the Gold Rush Cemetery.

Opposite page, lower left: Visitors explore the Gold Rush Dredge north of town. Part of the excursion is a chance to pan for gold. Opposite page, middle: Not much is left of Dyea.

Opposite page, bottom: The first gift shops served a clientele of Klondike gold-seekers in 1897.

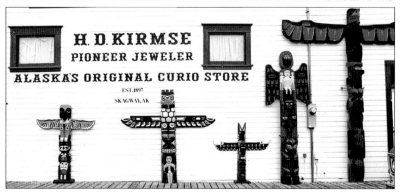

Skagway Excursions

(Subject to seasonal changes.)

Skagway & the Dangerous Days of '98
Klondike Summit & Liarsville Experience
Klondike Summit, Bridge, & Salmon Bake
Historical Tour & Liarsville Salmon Bake
Skagway's Original Street Car
To the Summit
Experience the Yukon
White Pass Scenic Railway
Best of Skagway
Klondike Scenic Highlights
Delectable Jewell Gardens
Deluxe Klondike Experience & Rail Adventure
Alaska Garden & Gourmet Tour
Yukon Jeep Adventure
Horseback Riding Adventure
Klondike Bicycle Tour

Rainforest Bicycle Tour
Klondike Rock Climbing & Rappelling
Alaska Sled Dog & Musher's Camp
Chilkoot Trail Hike & Float Adventure
Glacier Point Wilderness Safari
Glacier Lake Kayak & Scenic Railway
Dog Sledding & Glacier Flightseeing
Glacier Discovery By Helicopter
Heli-Hike & Rail Adventure
Alaska Nature & Wildlife Expedition
Remote Coastal Nature Hike
Takshanuk Mountain Trail by 4x4
Eagle Preserve Wildlife River Adventure
Chilkoot Lake Freshwater Fishing
Wilderness Kayak Experience
Skagway's Custom Classic Cars
Glacier Country Flightseeing

The Great Klondike Gold Rush

S ome 100,000 people set out for The Klondike. Only 30,000 to 40,000 of them actually made it. Of those who reached the goldfields, a small number stuck gold. But everyone brought back grand tales of The North.

Top: Well-wishers in San Francisco send off a ship after news spread across the U.S. about the steamship Portland arriving in Seattle in July, 1897 with a load of prospectors and their gold. UW Partridge

Left, middle: Look at these faces of prospectors aboard a Yukon River paddlewheeler, circa 1898. UW Thwaites 0394-1286

Above: A steep stretch of trail known as the "Golden Staircase" on the Chilkoot Pass. To enter Canada at the top of the pass, gold-seekers were required to have with them about 2,000 pounds of supplies. UW Hegg 100

Left, bottom: After getting over the pass in winter, prospectors wintered at Lake Bennett, where they cut down trees to make boats for the 500-mile trip down the Yukon River to Klondike. AMRC b64-1-43

Glacier Bay: Into The Ice!

Few things that you will see on your trip are as dramatic as going into the ice for the first time. When the first cruise ships came to the Bay in the 1880s, their favorite was Muir Glacier which calved 12 or 15 big bergs an hour, and passengers would go ashore and climb ladders to walk around on top.

Muir Glacier has long since retreated far up its fjord, and today most ships travel to Grand Pacific and Margarie Glaciers in Tarr Inlet. These calve far less, but the sight is no less dramatic!

Look carefully at the dotted lines and the dates on the map. In just 220 years, a blink of an eye in geologic time, a stunningly immense amount of ice has disappeared. Top: DK

British Columbia, Canada

In the 1950s Grand Pacific Glacier was receding slowly toward Canada. Mining interests got excited about building a port in Glacier Bay to export ore. But then the Glacier started moving forward again and their dreams ended.

Grand Pacific Glacier

Tarr Inlet

Rendu Inlet

137 00

59 00

Johns Hopkins Glacier

Johns Hopkins Inlet

Jaw Pt.

Muir Glacier

1879

Reid Inlet

Queen Inlet

Wachusett Inlet

1948

Harbor seals like to have their young on the ice floes here; when they are present, vessel traffic is prohibited.

Reid Glacier

Ships will often take a loop past the austere landscape of Queen Inlet.

Hugh Miller Inlet

Tidal Inlet

1907

1892

Adams Inlet

Muir Inlet

John Muir's famous adventure with the dog, Stikeen, took place on this glacier.

1860

Glacier Bay

Geikie Inlet

Glacier Bay National Park

Born from the Ice - the remarkable thing about Glacier Bay is this: when Captain Vancouver passed in 1794, there was no bay - just ice. By the time the next white man, John Muir, in 1879, saw it, the ice had retreated almost 30 miles!

58 40

1885 - The First cruise ships always went to very active Muir Glacier, until the earthquake of 1898. It shattered the Muir, which quickly retreated up its inlet.
Plus.. the passengers would go ashore where ladders would allow them to climb to the top of the Glacier and walk around! Imagine what the Park Service would do if a cruise line did that today!

Berg Bay

As recently as the 1960s, icebergs were a major hazard to navigation in Icy Strait. However in more recent years, most bergs melt before they drift out of Glacier Bay

58 20

Glacier Bay
6 Miles

Taylor Bay

Dundas Bay

Ice limits in various years.

136 00

Cross Sound

Cape Spencer

Inian Islands

1794

1000

Icy Strait

Bartlett Cove - Lodge and Park Headquarters.

Glacier Bay Wildlife

Top: Brown bear claws mussels off the rocks. Keep your binoculars handy. Bears are likely to appear on the hillsides above the bay as moving dots, as they gather berries. If the tide is low, you may see them along the shore as well. Ki Whorton

Left: For reasons not fully understood, Glacier Bay is also an excellent place for whale-watching. If you are exceptionally lucky you may see a breach like this one. Minden Pictures

Left, bottom: Seals are commonly seen on ice floes throughout Glacier Bay. So many use the ice calving from John Hopkins Glacier to birth their young that that part of the bay is closed during the summer. If your ship goes in there, consider yourself lucky, as it is one of the most dramatic areas in the whole Bay. DK

Below: Look on the steepest slopes for mountain goats like this one. You will be surprised at their ability to move around on incredibly steep terrain. DK

"We turned and sailed away, joining the out-going bergs, while "Gloria in Excelsis" seemed to be sounding all over the white landscape, and our burning hearts were ready for any fate, feeling that, whatever the future might hold, the tresures we had gained this glorious morning would enrich our lives forever."

John Muir's Bay

John Muir was a late 19th Century glaciologist/conservationist whose theory that Yosemite was formed by glaciers was at odds with the belief of geologists of his era. Hearing that there were glaciers in recently purchased Alaska, Muir set out in a big cedar canoe with Native paddlers from Wrangell in October, 1879 to see the big ice for himself.

When he arrived, his native paddlers were frightened, never having seen a place without trees. He charmed them into continuing on and so entered Glacier Bay, which had emerged from the ice only a few decades earlier.

He was stunned by what he found and immediately knew that what he saw confirmed his Yosemite theories, which were then reluctantly accepted by geologists.

Muir kept coming back to Alaska again and again, and his powerful prose about his experiences was both some of the best-ever written about Alaska and the impetus for the first cruise ships taking visitors into the ice.

Left, middle: Overlooking Muir Glacier, circa 1890
Bottom, left: Muir party, circa 1888
Below: Steamer Queen at the Muir, circa 1892.

Hoonah and Icy Strait Point

Top: Like many Alaska small towns, the fish plant is the main economic driver. These are trollers at Hoonah Cold Storage on a gorgeous summer evening.

Left: early photos around Hoonah.

Opposite top: A zip-line rider with Icy Strait Point (the old Hoonah Packing Company cannery) below. This particular zip has six parallel lines and is the longest ride of any zip line in Alaska. The ride ends at a restaurant, so you can catch a bite as well.

Opposite left: There is a pleasant short walk through the rain forest between the Cannery and the Landing Zone Bar and Grill. Easy wide path, definitely worth doing!

W
hen it opened in 2003, Icy Strait Point was unique among Alaska cruise ports. Ship visits are limited to one at a time, and the facility—a renovated cannery next to a Tlingit Indian village—is surrounded by wilderness. If you've cruised Alaska before, you know how congested the other towns can be with four or five ships in port at once. A visit here is a welcome change.

Passengers come ashore by lighter. The main feature is the cannery dock, which has a museum, cafe/restaurant, and numerous shops. Cannery life was a major cultural and economic element in coastal Alaska, and this is an excellent chance to get a close look. There are walking trails and a shuttle bus to nearby Hoonah, the largest Tlingit village in Alaska. The facility is owned by a Native corporation, which has preserved the rich Tlingit culture throughout.

Icy Strait Point is located in Port Frederick, just across Icy Strait from the entrance to Glacier Bay.

Exploring Sitka

Consider yourself lucky if your ship stops here. The lack of a cruise ship dock (all but very small cruise ships anchor and use lighters to send passengers ashore) and a location slightly off the beaten path make for a more mellow downtown than Ketchikan, Juneau, or Skagway.

Sitka was the capital when Alaska was part of Russia from the late 1700s until 1867. With brutal efficiency, sometimes slaughtering whole villages of natives if they didn't hunt for them, the Russians forced natives to hunt and kill sea otters for their valuable fur. Those furs created an empire that stretched from the Aleutians all the way down to Northern California.

Those were good years when Sitka was the busiest port on the Northwest Coast. Its residents drank fine wines and enjoyed ballet, when Ketchikan was a native village and Juneau was ice and snow.

After the Russians quickly slaughtered the sea otters almost to extinction, and Moscow was humiliated by Britain and France in the Crimean war in the 1850s, Russia was almost broke, and approached the US about selling Alaska. It was a great deal for the US: $7.2 million, about 2 cents an acre, done in 1867.

However the purchase was ridiculed as Seward's Folly or Seward's Icebox (William Seward being the Secretary of State at the time). Critics were silenced when gold was discovered.

After the Americans took over, Sitka slowly evolved into a sleepy fishing and logging town on the ocean side of Baranof Island.

In more modern times, Sitka's economy depended on the big plywood mill out in Sawmill Cove, and on commercial fishing. The closure of the mill in 1992 was a major financial blow to the town. But instead of languishing, Sitka experienced a slow renaissance based on the arts and, to a lesser degree, tourism.

Today, having missed the booms and busts of the gold rush, Sitka has become the cultural center of SE Alaska.

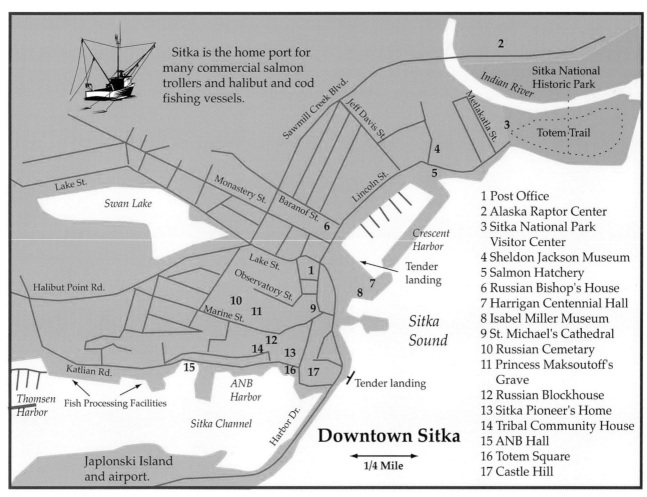

Sitka is the home port for many commercial salmon trollers and halibut and cod fishing vessels.

Sitka National Historic Park

Indian River

Totem Trail

Sawmill Creek Blvd.

Jeff Davis St.

Metlakatla St.

2

3

4

5

Lake St.

Monastery St.

Baranof St.

Lincoln St.

Swan Lake

Crescent Harbor

Tender landing

6

Lake St.

Observatory St.

1

7

8

Halibut Point Rd.

Marine St.

10

11

9

Sitka Sound

12

13

14

15

16

17

Katlian Rd.

Tender landing

Thomsen Harbor

Fish Processing Facilities

ANB Harbor

Sitka Channel

Harbor Dr.

Downtown Sitka

Japlonski Island and airport.

1/4 Mile

1 Post Office
2 Alaska Raptor Center
3 Sitka National Park
  Visitor Center
4 Sheldon Jackson Museum
5 Salmon Hatchery
6 Russian Bishop's House
7 Harrigan Centennial Hall
8 Isabel Miller Museum
9 St. Michael's Cathedral
10 Russian Cemetary
11 Princess Maksoutoff's
   Grave
12 Russian Blockhouse
13 Sitka Pioneer's Home
14 Tribal Community House
15 ANB Hall
16 Totem Square
17 Castle Hill

A Volcanic Prank

Mount Edgecumbe looms over Sitka, a prominent landfall in the days when ships from Asia came to load plywood from the now-closed mill. The volcano has been dormant for about 4,000 years.

Early on April Fool's Day, 1974, local prankster "Porky" Bickar loaded around 100 old car tires into a helicopter and flew up to the top of the volcano in pre-dawn darkness, set them alight to create a dramatic smoky fire, and spray-painted "Happy April Fool's Day" in 50-foot letters around the crater. Then he flew back to town and spread the word that Mount Edgecumbe was erupting.

P. 78 right: Tlingit Carver Tommy Joseph works at Sitka National Historical Park, a short walk along the water to the right as you come ashore. He and his team of carvers created the newest totem on display outside.

P. 79: Close to the ocean, Sitka is a major commercial fishing center. It is also probably the best place if you want to take a charter boat out and try to catch a king or a silver salmon.

Top: A young violinist welcomes visitors to Sitka.

Opposite top: Great scenery and protected waters make Sitka a good place to try sea kayaking.

Opposite lower left: The New Archangel Dancers perform traditional Russian dances when ships are in town.

Opposite lower right: Gray owl at The Raptor Center.

A really nice walk is off the lighters, then right along the shore to the Sitka National Historical Park, through the woods with totems here and there among the trees, left on Sawmill Creek Road, and then right up the driveway to the The Raptor Center.

Sitka Excursions
(Subject to seasonal changes)

Russian America History Tour
Russian America & Raptor Center Tour
Sitka Nature & History Walk
Sitka Bike & Hike Tour
Advanced Bike Adventure
Tongass Rainforest Hike
4x4 Wilderness Adventure
Sitka Sport-fishing
Wilderness Sea Kayaking Adventure
Dry Suit Snorkel Adventure
Sea Life Discovery Semi-Submersible
Sea Otter & Wildlife Quest
Sea Otter Quest & Alaska Raptor Center
Silver Bay Nature Cruise & Hatchery Tour
Wildlife Quest & Beach Trek
Alaska Up-Close Exclusive Cruise Adventure

The Unfriendly Shore

Mariners tread cautiously here. They know they will not find harbors with easy access when the wind blows, except for a few bays just north of Cape Spencer. This is the outside coast: bold, rugged, and flanked by the windy Gulf of Alaska on one side and the stunning and rugged St. Elias Range on the other. Take the time to go on deck with your binoculars. No other coast in North America is like this.

Look for La Perouse Glacier at **Mile 1060**. With its almost perpendicular 200- to 300-foot face, it's an outstanding landmark along this section of coast. This is an active glacier. As recently as 1997, it was advancing into the ocean, after having receded far enough to allow foot passage across the face at low tide.

To the east is mostly wilderness, a vast region from the coast up over the Fairweather Range and into Canada's Yukon Territory almost to the Alaska Highway. It does present, however, an opportunity for kayakers or rafters willing to find their adventures far from support and supplies

East and north of Hubbard Glacier is an area that has been nicknamed "The Roof of North America"—an immense rock, ice, and snow world with many of the continent's highest peaks. Ten thousand-footers are common here, and there are at least four higher than 15,000 feet.

Much of this area is the Wrangell-St. Elias National Park and Wilderness. This mountain wall catches the wet, eastward-flowing air, creating heavy snow. The immense weight of the snow pack creates the largest glaciers on the entire Pacific coast. Hubbard Glacier is part of a vast ice mass that extends parallel to the coast in an unbroken line, except for two places, almost 400 miles to Anchorage. Today, the glaciers all have receded substantially back from the shore, but a century ago, the ice reached the ocean in many places.

Top: French Explorer La Perouse lost 21 of his crew when the ebbing tide sucked their small boats into the tide rip known as "The Chopper."
Right: View of Cenotaph Island looking east. Wayne Parks photo

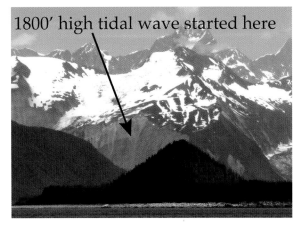
1800' high tidal wave started here

Terror at Lituya Bay

When something awakened commercial fisherman Howard Ulrich the evening of August 9, 1958, he stared out his window in amazement. The mountains at the head of the bay were jumping in an earthquake that knocked the needle off a seismograph 1,000 miles away. Next, an entire mountainside collapsed, creating a tidal wave that stripped the forest off to bare rock up to 1,800 feet above sea level!

As he watched, the tidal wave, having settled to "only" 50 feet high, headed for his anchored boat. Putting a life jacket on his six-year-old, he started the engine and headed directly into the wave. He knew this was his only chance to survive. Luckily, his anchor chain snapped and the wave carried him over the nearby trees on the spit, and out into the Pacific Ocean beyond. Two other boats weren't so lucky. One sank, but the crew was rescued. The other disappeared; all aboard were lost.

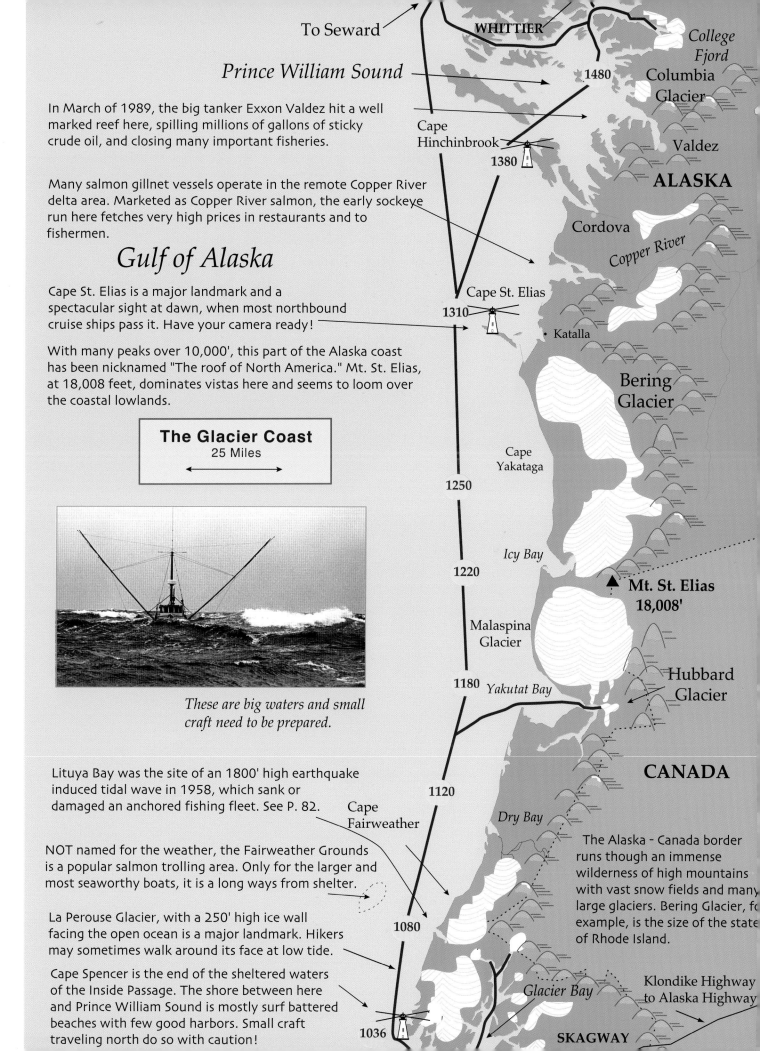

To Seward

WHITTIER

Prince William Sound

College Fjord

Columbia Glacier

In March of 1989, the big tanker Exxon Valdez hit a well marked reef here, spilling millions of gallons of sticky crude oil, and closing many important fisheries.

Cape Hinchinbrook

1480

1380

Valdez

ALASKA

Many salmon gillnet vessels operate in the remote Copper River delta area. Marketed as Copper River salmon, the early sockeye run here fetches very high prices in restaurants and to fishermen.

Cordova

Copper River

Gulf of Alaska

Cape St. Elias is a major landmark and a spectacular sight at dawn, when most northbound cruise ships pass it. Have your camera ready!

Cape St. Elias

1310

• Katalla

With many peaks over 10,000', this part of the Alaska coast has been nicknamed "The roof of North America." Mt. St. Elias, at 18,008 feet, dominates vistas here and seems to loom over the coastal lowlands.

Bering Glacier

The Glacier Coast
25 Miles

Cape Yakataga

1250

Icy Bay

1220

▲ **Mt. St. Elias 18,008'**

These are big waters and small craft need to be prepared.

Malaspina Glacier

1180 *Yakutat Bay*

Hubbard Glacier

CANADA

Lituya Bay was the site of an 1800' high earthquake induced tidal wave in 1958, which sank or damaged an anchored fishing fleet. See P. 82.

Cape Fairweather

1120

Dry Bay

NOT named for the weather, the Fairweather Grounds is a popular salmon trolling area. Only for the larger and most seaworthy boats, it is a long ways from shelter.

The Alaska - Canada border runs though an immense wilderness of high mountains with vast snow fields and many large glaciers. Bering Glacier, for example, is the size of the state of Rhode Island.

La Perouse Glacier, with a 250' high ice wall facing the open ocean is a major landmark. Hikers may sometimes walk around its face at low tide.

1080

Cape Spencer is the end of the sheltered waters of the Inside Passage. The shore between here and Prince William Sound is mostly surf battered beaches with few good harbors. Small craft traveling north do so with caution!

1036

Klondike Highway to Alaska Highway

Glacier Bay

SKAGWAY

College Fjord and Prince William Sound

The hidden jewel of Prince William Sound is College Fjord. Within an eight- mile stretch at the upper end, five major tidewater glaciers reach the water.

While Glacier Bay emerged from the ice so recently that big trees haven't grown up close to the ice, College Fjord is a place where the forest and the glaciers have co-existed for centuries.

This is the place where you are most likely to see sea otters. A good place to look is on top of ice floes, where you may see them with their young.

Above: Sea otter in classic pose. DK

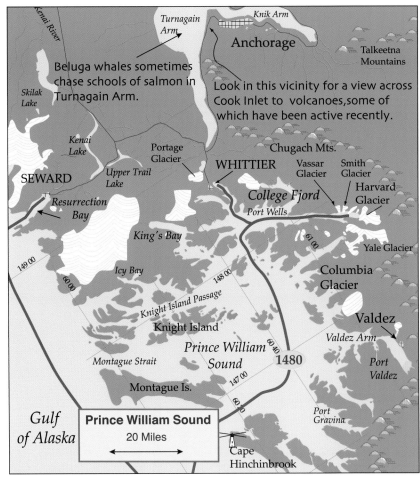

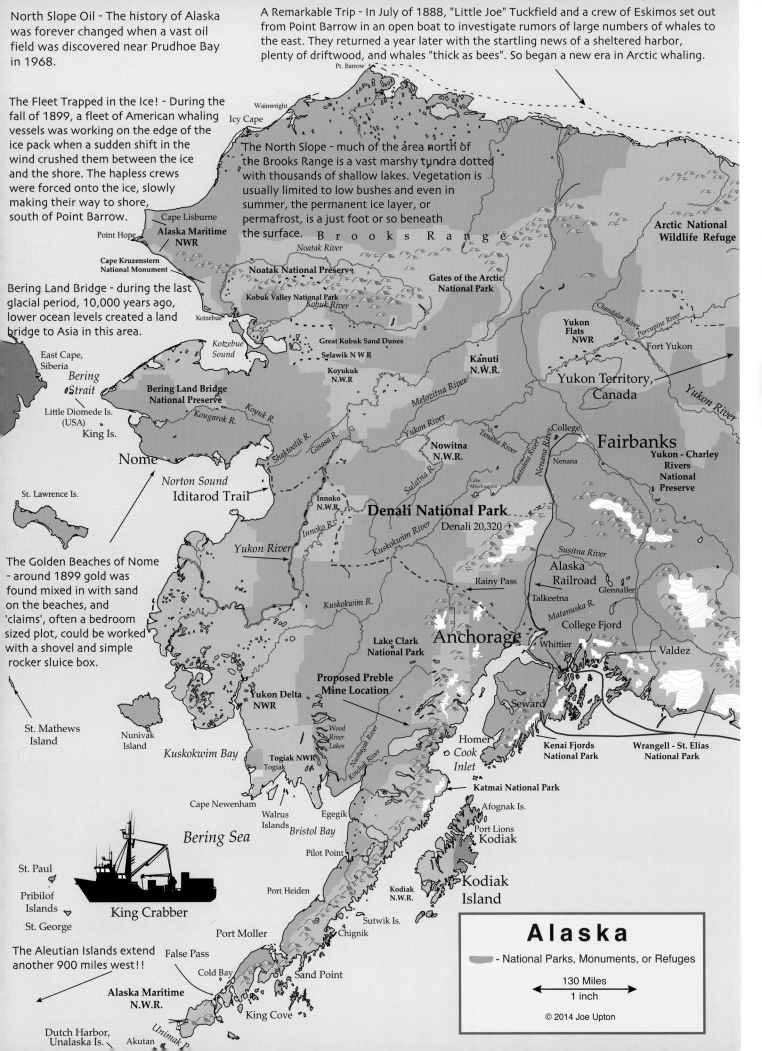

North Slope Oil - The history of Alaska was forever changed when a vast oil field was discovered near Prudhoe Bay in 1968.

A Remarkable Trip - In July of 1888, "Little Joe" Tuckfield and a crew of Eskimos set out from Point Barrow in an open boat to investigate rumors of large numbers of whales to the east. They returned a year later with the startling news of a sheltered harbor, plenty of driftwood, and whales "thick as bees". So began a new era in Arctic whaling.

The Fleet Trapped in the Ice! - During the fall of 1899, a fleet of American whaling vessels was working on the edge of the ice pack when a sudden shift in the wind crushed them between the ice and the shore. The hapless crews were forced onto the ice, slowly making their way to shore, south of Point Barrow.

The North Slope - much of the area north of the Brooks Range is a vast marshy tundra dotted with thousands of shallow lakes. Vegetation is usually limited to low bushes and even in summer, the permanent ice layer, or permafrost, is a just foot or so beneath the surface.

Bering Land Bridge - during the last glacial period, 10,000 years ago, lower ocean levels created a land bridge to Asia in this area.

The Golden Beaches of Nome - around 1899 gold was found mixed in with sand on the beaches, and 'claims', often a bedroom sized plot, could be worked with a shovel and simple rocker sluice box.

The Aleutian Islands extend another 900 miles west!!

Pt. Barrow
Wainwright
Icy Cape
Cape Lisburne
Point Hope
Alaska Maritime NWR
Cape Kruzenstern National Monument
Kotzebue
East Cape, Siberia
Bering Strait
Little Diomede Is. (USA)
King Is.
Nome
St. Lawrence Is.
Norton Sound
Iditarod Trail
St. Mathews Island
Nunivak Island
Kuskokwim Bay
Yukon Delta NWR
Togiak NWR
Togiak
Cape Newenham
Walrus Islands
Bristol Bay
Egegik
Pilot Point
Port Heiden
St. Paul
Pribilof Islands
St. George
Bering Sea
King Crabber
Port Moller
False Pass
Cold Bay
Sand Point
Chignik
Sutwik Is.
Kodiak N.W.R.
King Cove
Dutch Harbor, Unalaska Is.
Akutan
Unimak P.

B r o o k s   R a n g e
Noatak River
Noatak National Preserve
Kobuk Valley National Park
Kobuk River
Great Kobuk Sand Dunes
Selawik N W R
Koyukuk N.W.R
Gates of the Arctic National Park
Kanuti N.W.R.
Kotzebue Sound
Bering Land Bridge National Preserve
Kougarok R.
Koyuk R.
Shaktoolik R.
Gisasa R.
Innoko N.W.R.
Innoko R.
Yukon River
Kuskokwim River
Nowitna N.W.R.
Sulatna R.
Melozitna River
Yukon River
Tanana River
Nenana River
Kantishna River
Lake Minchumina
College
Fairbanks
Nenana
Denali National Park
Denali 20,320 +
Arctic National Wildlife Refuge
Chandalar River
Porcupine River
Fort Yukon
Yukon Flats NWR
Yukon Territory, Canada
Yukon River
Yukon - Charley Rivers National Preserve
Susitna River
Alaska Railroad
Talkeetna
Glennallen
Rainy Pass
Matanuska R.
College Fjord
Anchorage
Whittier
Valdez
Seward
Kuskokwim R.
Lake Clark National Park
Proposed Preble Mine Location
Wood River Lakes
Nushagak River
Kvichak River
Homer
Cook Inlet
Kenai Fjords National Park
Wrangell - St. Elias National Park
Katmai National Park
Afognak Is.
Port Lions
Kodiak
Kodiak Island

Alaska

▬ - National Parks, Monuments, or Refuges

◀─── 130 Miles ───▶
1 inch

© 2014 Joe Upton

Western Alaska is mostly roadless. Travel is by plane, boat, snowmobile, and even dogsled occasionally. The invention of the snowmobile around 1960 transformed winter transportation in much of The North. Before snowmobiles, many Natives in remote areas had to keep large teams of dogs, catch and dry fish to feed them, and take care of them for the rest of the year in order to have them for winter travel.

The land is dotted with tiny roadless Native communities. Life is often a struggle with income from seasonal construction jobs and fishing often not enough to last through the long winter.

A very large part of this land is tundra—wide areas of spongy wetland dotted by shallow ponds. In the darkness of the long winters, all this land sleeps. But the Arctic spring begins an awakening process that transforms The North.

The great flyways bring millions of migrating birds to the vast delta country of the Yukon, Kuskokwim, and smaller rivers. The long days cause vegetation of all sorts to grow at a rate not seen elsewhere.

Top: Aniachak Volcano with its steam vent looms over the Ugashik River.

Right, middle: Coffee Point Airport on the Egegik River in Bristol Bay. In such places, aviation gasoline is often delivered in drums by barge in the spring. The plane is a Piper Super Cub with tundra tires, probably used for spotting fish.

Right, bottom: Part of the endless tundra

Cap Thomsen and The Aleutian Mailboat

In the 1950s, the only outside contact for many Native villages on the Alaska Peninsula and into the remote Aleutian Islands was the 115-foot mail boat *Expansion*, which made regular round trips from Seward to Adak, skippered by her owner, Niels "Cap" Thomsen. Thomsen was one of those entrepreneurs Alaska seems to attract. In his earlier years, he operated a freight boat between Seattle and Ketchikan. Radar was expensive and rarely found on work boats then, but "Cap" impressed his waterfront investors when he cruised past their houses with his radar antenna turning. Little did they know that the antenna was all that he could afford, and that his son was turning it by hand.

When Thomsen got the mail-boat contract, the first thing he noticed was how some villages seemed to have a lot of single young men, and others, maybe just 40 or 50 miles way, might have way more single women. But without radio communications, neither group was aware of the other.

"So, I bought a Polaroid camera, and started taking pictures of all the singles in all the villages on my route," Thomsen recalled in an interview years later. "I would write their names on the photos, like 'Nina Popalook, Gambrel Bay, etc.' Then, I put up two bulletin boards, and I'd post the single gals on one and the single guys on the other.

"Pretty soon after that the word got out, and any time we'd come around the point to enter some harbor where there was a native village, you'd see the singles running down to the shore and rowing out as fast as they could to meet us, even before we had the anchor down—just to see if there was anything new on the singles bulletin boards!

-*"Cap" Niels Peter Thomsen.*

Top, left: Icing up was always a problem as these photos show. After a winter trip "to Westward," the Expansion is barely recognizable as a boat.
Opposite page: A final resting place in the Aleutian Islands

Voices From Denali

"...The storm now became so severe that I was actually afraid to get new dry mittens out of my rucksack, for I knew my hands would be frozen in the process... The last period of our climb is like the memory of an evil dream. La Voy was completely lost in the ice mist, and Professor Parker's frosted form was an indistinct blur above me... The breath was driven from my body and I held to my axe with stooped shoulders to stand against the gale; I couldn't go ahead. As I brushed the frost from my glasses and squinted upward through the stinging snow, I saw a sight that will haunt me to my dying day. The slope above me was no longer steep! That was all I could see. What it meant I will never know for certain—all I can say is that we were close to the top."
— Belmore Browne, *The Conquest of Mt. McKinley*

"I was snowshoeing along about fifty feet back of the sled, with Harry (Liek) right behind me when, without warning, the snow fell away under my snowshoes. I plunged into sudden darkness.

"I had time to let out a feeble shout. Then for a couple of long, long seconds I plummeted downward. I remember thinking, 'This is it, fellow!' Then my pack scraped against the side of the crevasse, my head banged hard against the ice wall, and I came to a jarring stop.

"When my head cleared and I could look around in the blue darkness, I saw I was on a plug of snow wedged between the ice walls. On either side, this wedge of snow fell away into sheer blackness.

"About forty feet above me I could see a ray of sunlight, slanting through the hole I had made in the surface crust. The crevasse was about twelve feet wide up there, it narrowed to two feet down where I was. Below was icy death."
— Grant Pearson, *My Life of High Adventure*

Tragedy On The Mountain

Top: Members of the 1932 Lindley - Liek Expedition, returning from the first successful climb to both summits, found an empty camp. It belonged to Theodore Koven and Alan Carpe, who had been flown onto Muldrow Glacier by legendary pilot Joe Crossman. The pair were there to make cosmic ray observations and were thrilled that Crossman had been able to make the first glacier landing on Denali to drop them.

Exploring nearby, the members of the Lindley - Liek Expedition, already exhausted by climbing for almost 36 hours straight, found Koven's frozen body. Footprints indicated that Koven and Carp had probably fallen through the snow into a crevasse, and that Koven, unable to rescue his partner, managed to climb out, but succumbed to his injuries and perished from hypothermia.

Above: Harry Liek and Alfred Lindley after the climb. Liek was Superintendent of Mt. Mckinley National Park. UAF Rasmusen Library photos.

"There was no pride of conquest.... Rather...that a privileged communion with the high places of the earth had been granted... secret and solitary since the world began. All the way down, unconscious of weariness in the descent, my thoughts were occupied with the glorious scene my eyes gazed upon, and should gaze upon never again."

First coming to Alaska as an eight-year old on a sightseeing trip, Belmore Browne became an important figure in Alaska climbing as well as a significant wildlife painter.

Browne was part of the 1906 Denali expedition when the leader, Frederick Cook, sent his crew away, and claimed to have reached the top solo.

Browne doubted that he had and went on another expedition four years later that found that Cook's photographic "proof" was in fact of another peak, 20 miles away from Denali.

As the quote on the left reveals, Browne came very very close (about 125') to the top on his third attempt in 1912. ASL PCA 01-3441

"But in half an hour, we stood on the narrow edge of the spur top, facing failure. Here, where the black ridge leading to the tops of the pink cliffs should have flattened, all was absolutely sheer, and a hanging glacier, bearded and dripping with bergschrunds, filled the angle in between... I heard Fred say, 'It ain't that we can't find a way that's possible, taking chances. There ain't no way.'

"We were checkmated with steepness, at 11,300 feet with eight days of mountain food on our hands. But remember this: also with scarce two weeks provisions below with which to reach the coast and winter coming. The foolishness of the situation, and the fascination, lies in the fact that except in this fair weather, unknown in Alaska at this season, we might have perished either night in those two exposed camps."

— Robert Dunn, *Shameless Diary of an Explorer*

"We tried to take some snaps, but had to give it up. For four minutes only did I leave my mittens off, and in that time, I froze five tips of my fingers to such a degree that after they had first been white, some weeks later, they turned black, and at last fell off, with the nails and all."

— Erling Strom, *How We Climbed Mt. McKinley*

"... My mind was racing. I had to grab the rock near Dave with my left hand; it was bare, no mitten or sock. It would be frozen. I had to. Suddenly my bare hand shot out to grab the rock. Slicing cold.

"I saw Dave's face, the end of his nose raw, frostbitten. His mouth, distorted into an agonized mixture of compassion and anger, swore at me to get a glove on. I looked at my hand. It was white, frozen absolutely white."

–Art Davidson, *Minus 148 Degrees, the Winter Ascent of Mt. McKinley*

Top quote by Hudson Stuck, in Mt. McKinley: The Pioneer Climbs *by Terris Moore*

The River Country

North and west of Fairbanks is the vast Alaska bush. This is river country. The majority of villages and settlements in the region between the Alaska Range and the Bering Sea and Arctic Ocean lie along one of the many rivers with Native and Russian names like Kitchatna, Tonzona, Kantishna, Hoholitna, and Chilikadrotna, Ugashik, Nushagak, and Kinak. When the sea ice recedes from shore during the summer, watercraft ranging from big tugs and barges to outboard jet boats move people and supplies around. When the ice is in, it is usually hard and smooth enough for vehicles.

Where there are no highways, the arrival of the first freight barge in the spring is always an exciting community event. This freight (usually in 40-foot containers or vans) often begins its journey from Seattle, stacked five and six high on a huge 400-foot ocean-going barge, towed by a 5,000-horsepower tug. Somewhere near the mouth of the Yukon River, perhaps at St. Michaels, the containers are hoisted onto a smaller barge, to be pushed upstream. Sometimes, for freight bound for villages on the smaller rivers, the container would be transferred a third time onto a yet smaller barge, pushed by an even smaller tug.

"Ice Out," before air travel, was a big event. Notices were posted around towns like Fairbanks to keep residents informed: "Ice moved at Fort Gibbon this morning at 8 a.m." This was important news because movement upriver of the first steamer of the season meant fresh vegetables, followed shortly thereafter by the "slaughterhouse boat" with its pens of cows, sheep, pigs, geese, and chickens brought up from Seattle.

Top: The paddlewheel excursion vessel, Discovery III, operating out of Fairbanks, offers a great way to get a flavor of the river country that dominates much of interior and western Alaska.

Opposite page: Discovery III passes a typical fish-wheel and Athabascan Indian "fish camp." The fish-wheel catches salmon, which the Natives smoke for winter.

Above: Float planes are the aerial equivalents of pickup trucks for many bush Alaskans.

Paddlewheeler Days

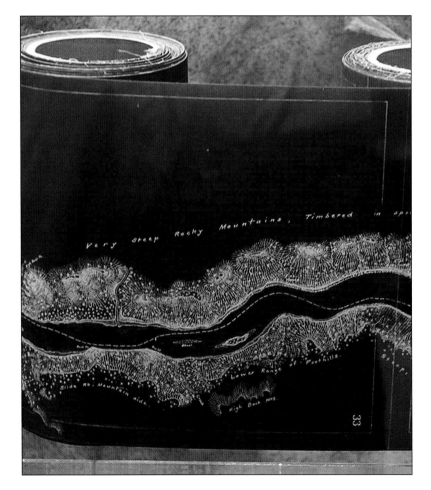

Top: Passengers leaving the steamer Tutsi at Ben-My-Chree, on the Upper Yukon, circa 1925.

Left: River channels changed frequently, so hand-drawn charts were created by the paddlewheeler captains and river pilots. This one of much of the river is taped together from many sheets, rolled back or forth as the trip demands.

Opposite page, top: Steamers would operate as late as possible each fall. Once the rivers froze, there would be little income for months. Sometimes a steamer such as this one would stay too late, becoming frozen in the ice. Yukon Archives

Opposite page, bottom: The steamer White Horse moving upriver in Five Finger Rapids on the Upper Yukon. This was a particularly challenging spot. Because the rapids were narrow and the current heavy, steamers needed plenty of power to get through. Under-powered vessels would run a line to shore and winch themselves through, aided by the paddlewheels turning at full speed ahead. This was the route used by the majority of the men who headed north to the Klondike Gold Rush in 1898. Only the wealthy could afford steamer passage with all their gear. Most built their own boats and floated down the river. UW21255

B efore the arrival of modern social services and the cash economy, winters in the far north could be another word for starvation if game was scarce.

In those days, the sea and land provided a hard living. The result was a remarkably tough and resilient people. In boats made of walrus hides stitched together and stretched over driftwood frames, they traveled hundreds of miles to hunt bowhead and other whales. Other hunters waited for hours by holes in the ice for a seal to surface briefly to breathe.

Housing was sod and earth huts, or igloos in winter, and skin tents when families moved to be closer to fish runs in the summer. When the white men came, Eskimos quickly learned about commerce and the value of their ivory carvings. As soon as the gold rush created settlements of whites in western Alaska, Eskimos began to camp nearby to carve and sell ivory.

Today's Eskimos are more apt to live in prefab houses delivered by barge and depend on seasonal fishing and construction work.

Above: "Summer Camp," a painting by Ken Lisbourne, Point Hope. Often Eskimos, especially those living near the deltas of the great Yukon and Kuskokwim rivers, would travel to campsites on the water where they could catch salmon and set up drying racks. In addition to preserving fish for themselves, they would often dry many chum salmon to feed their dog teams over the winter.

Right: Yu'pik Ircit, or human/fox mask, from the author's collection. Eskimo legend has it that Ircenrrat were extraordinary persons who appeared alternately as humans or small mammals. This would be revealed as footprints that would alternate between animal and human tracks.

Opposite page, top: "Shoppers" aboard a trading schooner, circa 1920. Each year, trading vessels would travel north to Bering Sea Eskimo villages loaded with supplies such as sewing machines, five-gallon tins of kerosene, Aladdin Lamps, fabric, rifles, and all manner of smaller items. Natives like these women would come aboard with skins or ivory to trade for supplies. UW17962

Opposite page, bottom: Ivory Carvers during the Nome Gold Rush. UW17963

The Unfriendly Bering Sea

The farther west you go, the bleaker the land becomes. In the Aleutians, trees bigger than a human are rarely seen. On the mainland, the land is mostly tundra and ponds, backed up by austere volcanos. On the eastern shore of the Bering Sea, good harbors are few; the shores are all scoured by the ice pack in winter, threatening docks and breakwaters. But underneath lies a rich fisheries resource that has been harvested by many nations for decades.

In deeper waters father offshore lie king crab, target of the "Deadliest Catch" fleet. Imposed by Congress in 1976, the 200-mile limit first allowed joint ventures: US boats fishing for foreign processor ships, and eventually this led to the development of sophisticated, high-tech U.S. fishing vessels such as the one above.

In the 1980's it was essentially a new gold rush as entrepreneurs rushed to get big ships built to operate in the new fisheries. Regulations were quickly put in place to control overfishing.

Ironically, the biggest money is made with the tiny roe sacs of the lowly pollock. A large fleet of large vessels has been developed for this fishery.

The hard part is simply that the Bering Sea is rough, dangerous, and cold for much of the year.

Top: Aleutian fun: a 300-foot trawler, Bering Sea, 2013. The vessel catches as well as processes fish.
Matthew Upton

Left, middle: King crabber Walter Kuhr with a deck-load of king crab, in the glory days of the fishery

Bottom left: Rough weather on our crabber, the Flood Tide, Bering Sea, 1971

A hundred thirty years after the first cannery was built on Bristol Bay in the eastern Bering Sea, the bay's fishery is still going strong. The few old-timers who still remember the sailboat days, a time prior to 1950 when only sailing vessels were allowed to fish the bay, shake their heads in wonder at what they see now.

Today, thanks to the 200-mile limit that kept foreign fleets from targeting U.S. Bristol Bay salmon, this is the strongest red salmon fishery in the world. But it's short and very intense. Each June, some 10,000 fishermen and 5,000 processing workers arrive to work the six-week season. The peak of the season lasts only about ten days, amid pressure to be in the right spot and keep your equipment and crew working. A good day fishing in the right place can represent ten percent of your catch for the entire season.

Top: Sailboat days—lines of sailing gillnetters being towed back from the fishing grounds. Pulling the nets by hand, rowing with 14-foot oars, and sailing in the choppy waters of the bay was tough work.

Right, middle: Intense action on "the line." Fishing areas are tightly regulated and boats fight to be right here where fish pour into the bay.

Right, bottom: Picking red salmon aboard your mapmaker's gillnetter, 1990. On the right is our son, now a maritime lawyer.

Effects of a Changing Climate

I t's completely beyond what any of our models had predicted."

"I never expected it to melt this fast."

Such were the comments from scientists at a recent symposium on the Arctic. There still may be debate in a few quarters about global warming, but not in Alaska—it's here.

The tidewater glaciers on the Alaska coast had been receding slowly for decades, even before global warming became a household word. But recent events in the Arctic and their implications for the future are sobering, especially for species dependent on wide areas of sea ice such as the polar bear.

Until a decade or so ago, sea ice covered most of the Arctic Ocean in winter, melting and receding a bit in the summer, and then refreezing quickly again each fall. But recently the sea ice has receded dramatically in the summer. From 1979 to 2000, the average area of ice in the Arctic Ocean was around three million square miles. By August of 2007, that number had shrunk by half, a truly staggering reduction. One scientist predicted that the Arctic would be ice free in summer by 2030.

It may happen sooner. As ice melts, the darker ocean absorbs much more heat than the white ice which reflects the sun's rays, further increasing the melting.

The climate change will create losers and winners. The Northwest Passage shipping route from Atlantic to Pacific would become reality. Vast new areas would be open for mineral and oil exploration. Valuable fish species such as salmon and pollock might thrive by moving their range farther north. The polar bear would probably be a loser. It depends on the ice pack for habitat.

Many Native villages in the Arctic are built close to the shore, but had been protected from storm seas by a natural barrier created by the ice. As the ice recedes, the seas become larger, and villages may either have to relocate or eventually be swept away. Permafrost–frozen earth close to the surface of the ground is another huge issue. Most small buildings and houses in the Arctic essentially have permafrost foundations. As the ice in soil melts, the buildings slowly settle into the soggy ground.

Can global warming be stopped? In theory, perhaps. But the realities of a rapidly developing Asia and a global economy built on high energy use make it unlikely.

So, if you want to see Alaska in its present state, go soon! *Alaskastock Photo*

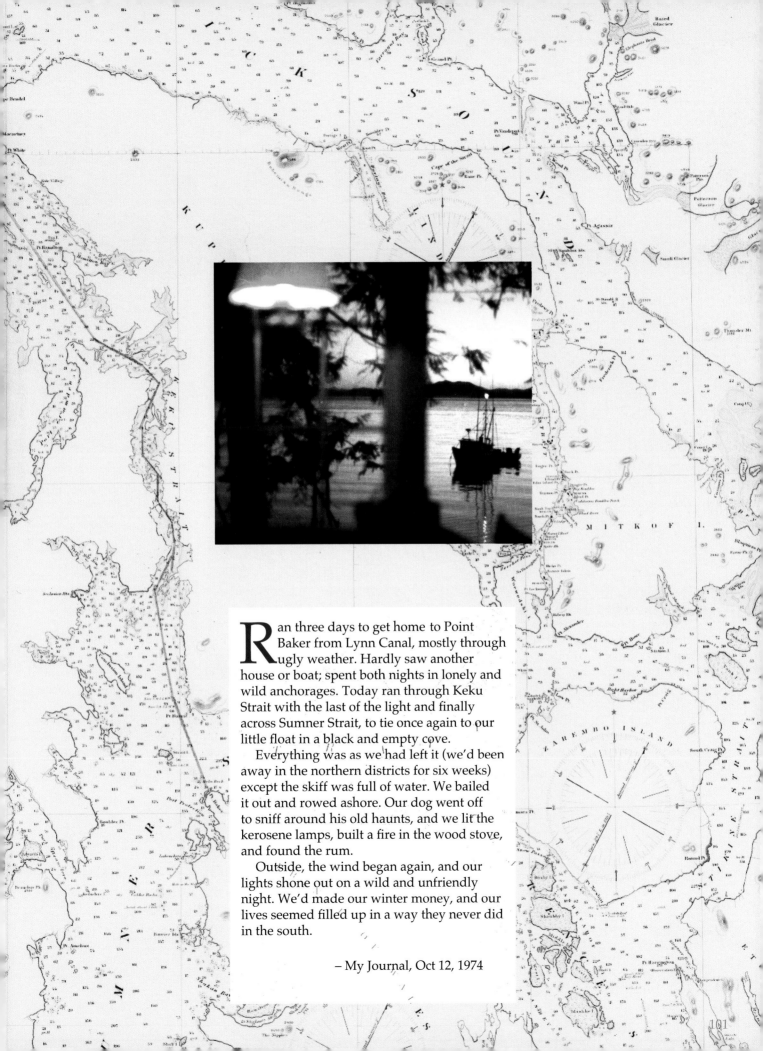

Ran three days to get home to Point Baker from Lynn Canal, mostly through ugly weather. Hardly saw another house or boat; spent both nights in lonely and wild anchorages. Today ran through Keku Strait with the last of the light and finally across Sumner Strait, to tie once again to our little float in a black and empty cove.

Everything was as we had left it (we'd been away in the northern districts for six weeks) except the skiff was full of water. We bailed it out and rowed ashore. Our dog went off to sniff around his old haunts, and we lit the kerosene lamps, built a fire in the wood stove, and found the rum.

Outside, the wind began again, and our lights shone out on a wild and unfriendly night. We'd made our winter money, and our lives seemed filled up in a way they never did in the south.

– My Journal, Oct 12, 1974